Wishing you.

Your einotes(?) ...

"Best day."

Best wishes,

Suzy & Adrian

For. Mike Paxton.

A PARTICULAR LUNN

With every good wish.

Mick Lunn.

20th May 1991

Stockbridge

A Particular Lunn

One Hundred Glorious Years on the Test

Mick Lunn

with

Clive Graham-Ranger

UNWIN

HYMAN

LONDON SYDNEY WELLINGTON

First published by Unwin Hyman Ltd, in 1990.

Unwin Hyman Limited
15–17 Broadwick Street, London W1V 1FP

Allen & Unwin Australia Pty Ltd
8 Napier Street, North Sydney, NSW 2060, Australia

Allen & Unwin New Zealand Pty in association with the
Port Nicholson Press
Compusales Building, 75 Ghuznee Street, Wellington, New Zealand

---

British Library Cataloguing in Publication Data

Lunn, Mick
A Particular Lunn: 100 glorious years on the River Test.
1. Hampshire. Test River, history. Social life, 1945.
Biographies
I. Lunn, Mick   II. Ranger, Clive Graham
942.2732085092

ISBN 0–04–440573–1

Typeset in 12/14 point Caslon by Nene Phototypesetters Ltd, Northampton
Printed by Butler & Tanner Ltd, Frome, Somerset

Contents

LIST OF PLATES

FOREWORD BY LORD PERTH, PRESIDENT OF THE HOUGHTON CLUB

WHEN I joined the Houghton Club forty years ago, Alf Lunn was in charge. He was a quieter man than his son Mick, but equally a friend to all Club members who would turn to him as the fount of wisdom on all things to do with dry fly, as indeed had been his father before him. Two years ago the Club celebrated their good fortune of 100 years of the Lunns – a feast and a presentation. Every year after our Annual General Meeting Mick joins us and his address – his review of the past year's activities, the problems we face, and the outlook for the coming year – puts us in good heart for the lunch that follows. He speaks well and manages to give a message of hope and cheer.

Having Mick with one any evening is probably worth two or more extra fish, but he is a hard taskmaster – no let up, no slackening in pursuit of the rising fish. All the same, every club member seeks his company, his keenness and his help. I recall how one very eminent member expected to have Mick every time by right when he came to fish. The then President had, diplomatically, to intervene.

Here I digress and tell my fishing story (or should it be Mick's?). Late of a May evening on the Black Lake beat we saw a salmon boil, no trout could move so much water. A shortening of the 3x line and the small salmon fly which I always kept against such a chance. The first cast and the fish was on my 8ft Hardy's split cane. The stream runs smooth and deep and the fish slowly wound its way down stream. Nothing could I do but follow, trying to keep the rod up. One hundred yards below was a footbridge across the stream and the fish decided to swim sedately under it. We somehow passed the rod under the 3ft wide bridge and the fish went on his way down the stream. A little further on the riverbank took a sharp left turn. That was the signal for the salmon to come back up again. I saw ahead of me an endless replay of passing the rod under the bridge, going up 100 yards and then back again under the bridge . . . and it was now getting dark. But Mick thought otherwise and called for my net. He stood on the bridge, net deep in the water, and as the fish proceeded majestically on its way it found it had put its head into it. Mick swirled fish and net towards the bank and somehow I got my arms around the two, and wet but triumphant scrambled to dry land, hugging the salmon, just like Mr Briggs as drawn by Leech long ago. Twenty and a half pounds in five minutes and a record in the Club's annals. My fish? Mick's fish? Anyhow our fish.

Having known Mick for forty years it does not surprise me that his book is both good and entertaining. Fishermen everywhere will be able to learn from it and enjoy its stories. One day I suspect it will be a collectors' classic, worthy of one, if not the greatest, of the chalk streams: the Test, and worthy of the three generations of Lunn.

Preface by Clive Graham-Ranger

As a teenager I passed through Stockbridge in Hampshire several times a year, on journeys from London to my birthplace in Durrington, Wiltshire, on the Upper Avon. I knew Stockbridge as the home of the Houghton Fishing Club on the famed Middle Test.

In later years I was fascinated by John Waller Hills's biography of William J. Lunn, the riverkeeper whose researches into the trout and the fly became something of a preoccupation and filled many hours on winter evenings. But I never imagined that I would meet William Lunn's grandson Mick, third generation riverkeeper, at the Grosvenor Hotel, Stockbridge, for more than a century the headquarters of the Houghton Club, and work with him on this book ... work together for eight months with never a cross word or disagreement between us.

Mick's enthusiasm for the Test and its plant and wildlife is catching: through his unbounded patience and knowledge I have thrilled at the sight of an orange tip butterfly; watched eagerly as a grey wagtail has hawked the first hatch of fly from the shallows at Sheepbridge, heralding a rise of trout; lifted into a 1 lb 4oz wild brown trout when I heard the Houghton 'You' from Mick at my elbow as the fish rose and slipped down my averagely-cast Little Brown Sedge.

We have to thank a number of people who, in no particular order, are:

Sanders Nicolson, for the lyrical colour photographs which fill many pages of this book; he photographed the Houghton Club waters day by day from an impossible 3am to dusk. As he would be the first to say: they are individually worth 1000 words of mine or anyone else's words.

Mark Flisher, who devoted much time, patience and skill to capture the unique atmosphere of the Houghton clubroom and its treasures in the Grosvenor Hotel, Stockbridge.

I would also like to thank my secretary, Tara Emmerson, and my wife,

Sue Blair, for undertaking the onerous task of transcribing the many conversations between Mick and me which formed the basis for the finished manuscript.

Finally, Mick and I would also like to thank our (fisherman) publisher Merlin Unwin, for his patience, encouragement and advice, and the members of the Houghton Club who allowed us to spend hours in their clubroom researching their history.

Stockbridge;
'Ganichou', Bordeaux, Gironde;
'Bralorne', Charlton Horethorne, Somerset;
London;
1990

To Sam Graham-Ranger and Mick's grandson, Ben.

I

A BOYHOOD ON THE TEST

———————◆◆◆———————

MY river, the Test, is not a large river, but it has been food and drink for man and beast since before history began; a highway for trade and travellers; power for dozens of mills; all these and more.

It rises in the village of Ashe near Overton and winds gracefully through Hampshire's chalk downlands until it reaches the sea at Southampton Water. Throughout its length, within the boundaries of one county, the Test even in its upper reaches is never a thin and trickling water as are so many of our rivers, because the Test is a chalkstream; the most famous chalkstream in England; famous for its secluded beauty, its placid, crystal clear glides and the trout that lurk in its depths.

Chalkstreams are not affected, as are more western and northern rivers, by the weather. It would take Moses' flood to disturb the calm, pellucid flow of the Test. That's because it is fed by the chalk reservoirs, or aquifers, deep under the downlands through which the river flows.

Hundreds of years ago the Test in winter was allowed to flood the water-meadows on either side to create fresh, green spring pastures; while year-round its never-ending flow powered the mills, which at one time bordered its length, grinding flour and driving the machinery in the fulling mills to provide the wool merchants of the southland with their wealth.

Standing here on the bridge above Sheepbridge Shallows, a few yards from Riverside Cottage in the village of Houghton, I take immense pride in the fact that three generations of riverkeeping Lunns have lived here for more than a century. For more than one hundred years the Lunns have been responsible for tending this beautiful river; nurturing it, understanding its ways, and responding to its every whim and fancy. In so doing we

1

Riverside Cottage, 1939

have been able to guarantee that the members of the Houghton Club – the most famous, if not the oldest, flyfishing club in the world – get the best sport from their 15 miles of the Middle Test.

It has been a challenging and rewarding task, a lifelong mission, which has been carried on from father to son, since 1887 when my grandfather, William J. Lunn, first arrived here at Riverside Cottage to take up his duties as keeper of the Houghton Club's famed waters.

As I look upstream through the avenue of rustling, silver-green willows, my eye is caught by the flutter of leaves on the aspen trees I helped to plant as a lad, thirty-odd years ago. I was born 300 yards from this spot with the sound of the river in my ears.

In more than sixty years, that sound has never been far away. Today, as then, the river's bank are filled with the subtle delicate colours and scented profusion of loosestrife, willow herb, agrimony, meadow sweet and comfrey. But from April to September, it is the trout which lure the members of the Houghton Club to this unspoiled and peaceful corner of rural England.

2

Myself (left) and Victor Speck outside Riverside Cottage, 1932

The trout of the Houghton Club signify their plump presence with an audible sipping sound, a lunging splash, or a silent kidney-shaped ring on the water, as they intercept the flies and nymphs of the Test which emerge by day and fall back to the water to lay their eggs in the evening. My childhood romance with this river and its magical lifecycle has never ceased to be a source of wonder and pleasure to me.

Born on 14 February 1926 I was, quite naturally, christened Valentine. It wasn't until I went to the local village school at Houghton, when I was five, that I began to realise I wasn't another Tom, Dick or Harry. But my name ceased to embarrass me when, at the age of seven, I entered the fancy dress

3

competition in the annual village fête as Mickey Mouse. I not only won first prize, but also earned the name Mick, which has stuck with me ever since. In fact, today there are only a couple of people in the village who call me Val. Mind you, with a name like Valentine nobody ever forgets your birthday.

The village of Houghton, where I grew up, was a very insular and self-sufficient place. Even though the next village was only 3 miles away, we never went there, it would have been like going abroad. Everybody in Houghton knew everybody else and their business, and as children we were pretty well all the best of friends.

There were only two buses a day – one there and one back – and the only real trip out was when my mother took the bus into Winchester on market days, taking me with her whether I wanted to go or not. I have to admit that all the bustle and noise was very alien to me and I couldn't wait to get home.

In those days, the church was the hub of village life. As a boy I sang in the choir, so in addition to matins and evensong every Sunday, I went to choir practice once a week. Sunday mornings, though, were special times because we village lads would gather in the graveyard and swap cigarette cards. At that time, several brands of cigarette had picture cards of footballers, cricketers, birds, and the like. After church we used to scoot round all the men in the village, cadge their cards and then swap them in an effort to build up a complete, fifty-card set.

Like all boys at that time, we were mad keen on football. Unfortunately, the village of Houghton could only raise ten boys to make up a team, so on match days we recruited Honor Burt, the blacksmith's daughter, to play on the wing. She was ten-tenths tomboy, she gave and expected no quarter and was always the first to join in the fight which seemed to end every match.

We weren't exactly angels and often played games like knock-down-ginger in the evenings. We would tie a piece of string to someone's door knocker, hide behind a hedge and pull the string. Scrumping, or stealing apples, and bird nesting were other pastimes, but you always had to have a good look round before you went down to the marsh or the water-meadows to make sure a keeper wasn't around.

The keepers were no different to my grandfather and father, but to us lads they always seemed a bit ogreish. And if I ever got caught, which fortunately didn't happen too often, I would get two telling-offs, one from the keeper and the other from my father. Father was quite a disciplinarian, but unlike other fathers in the village, he never took his belt to me.

One of the high points in the church calendar was the annual Sunday

School outing when all the children and their mothers would load into Cooper's old coach. The boot was filled with bottles of pop and a huge picnic, and we would motor off to Southampton where we'd get the steamer to Ryde on the Isle of Wight.

The village fête was another great thing for us. The night before the fête the fairground people would arrive with their dodgem cars, roundabouts and swings. There were also the preparations for the fancy dress competition, when mothers spent long hours making costumes for their children. In addition, there were lots of organised games, races of all sorts, bowling for a pig, best flower and vegetable competitions, drawing pictures, you name it . . . I remember winning first prize for the best flower arrangement, but it was easy for me because I had access to the river and all the wild flowers growing on its banks. I remember winning a bicycle race one year and I always came first in the 100 yard dash.

In 1936, when I was 10 years old, the village fête was held on Coronation Day and the main prizes were presented by Sir Lionel and Lady Wells, who lived at Houghton Lodge. They weren't exactly the lord and lady of the manor, but they did always sit in the front pew in church and their kneelers were embroidered. They were great beneficiaries of the village of Houghton, having paid for the building of the village hall.

Most months there were village dances, and as children, if we were really lucky we were invited. I really felt like Jack the Lad on those Saturday nights, especially if I managed to get a dance with Sylvia Russell or Phyllis Stone; they were the bee's knees.

On other weekend nights during the winter, the Women's Institute, of which mother was a staunch supporter, would hold small concert parties. My father was usually the master of ceremonies and mother was very good at comedy sketches. Bill the blacksmith would sing songs like 'A Long, Long Trail a Windin'' and 'Pack Up Your Troubles' and Reg Allam, the gamekeeper's son down at Bossington, played mouth organ duets with me. The star turn was Fred Shadwell, a farmer from the nearby Wallops, who told stories about the Local Defence Volunteers and the Home Guard. One tale I remember from all those years ago was about Bill Burt, the blacksmith, and Ken Potter, a carpenter, on night patrol. Out shouts a voice, 'Halt, who goes there?'

The reply, 'Friend,' comes back.

'Advance and be recognised,' calls Bill.

'Don't be a bloody fool,' shouts the voice, 'I'm the other side of the river.'

Riverside Cottage, where grandfather lived from the time he was made

Head Keeper in 1887 until his retirement in 1931, was the proverbial Shangri-la to me as a boy. The most impressive thing about it was the garden with its box hedges either side of the path, a filbert tree in the corner, a pear tree trained around the house and six apple trees: one for himself and grandmother and one planted at the birth of each of his four children. Only Aunty Bett's tree – a King Pippin – survives to this day; it always produced the best eaters of the six. Aunty Bett is still alive; 93 now and still going strong.

My grandfather, as I remember, was quite a good gardener – after all, when he was 16 he was one of the ten gardeners employed at a big house called High Ashurst, near Box Hill in Surrey – but he preferred the river, collecting this, catching that, experimenting with the other. He put up a special seat down by the river and would spend hour after hour sitting up there just looking; I think he preferred that to planting potatoes or trimming the hedges.

Grandmother and Rose seemed to do most of the work in the garden, although grandfather did plant a superb asparagus bed. His stock saying was, 'I'm always glad when it snows, then my garden looks as good as anyone's.' In those days you grew food for the table, so everybody gardened. I can remember to this day the winters when the air was heavy with the smell of bonfires after the general tidying up.

One of the special things in those days was an allotment where you could grow half an acre of potatoes. We were luckier than most because we knew all of the local farmers, so a load of manure was never a problem. Since those early days I have always taken pride in my own garden. It has almost been a matter of honour with me to keep it tidy. I believe that if a riverkeeper has a well looked after garden then his river tends to look nice; if his garden is untidy, more often than not, his river is also a bit of a mess.

Looking back, I suppose we were better off than other people in the village, because we had the right to shoot, fish and trap food for the table. It was quite a treat going around with my father, setting up the wires and catching rabbits. I also went ferreting in the afternoons after school as we were encouraged to combine completing our homework with various useful activities which included ferreting for rabbits, or taking the terriers out to catch rats underneath the turkey pens. After that I might milk a few cows with old Bill North – one of the Club's tenant farmers, who had a dairy farm down the road – and return home with a pail of milk as my reward. Then it never seemed like work because I felt that if people allowed me to milk their cows, they must have thought I was pretty grown up. The only problem was there are just two things you can make with milk: custard and rice pudding and I sure had my fill of rice pudding when I was a lad.

Apart from the allotment potatoes and the odd pail of milk, we mostly lived off the land and the river. We used to eat pike and grayling, and during the Second World War, when meat was rationed, we ate a lot of water birds. Mother's specialities included moorhen and coot casserole. There were also plenty of game birds about, what with the pheasant and the odd wild duck that made the mistake of flying over father's gun. But as a boy, one of the high points was fishing for pike, some of which grew very large, having spent their lives feeding off our carefully-reared trout.

Although we often used grayling as bait, the best fish you could have as pike bait was roach, because it stayed on the hook well and the silver sheen of its body showed up well in the water; pike found them irresistible. We caught most of our roach in the Marshcourt Peat Pits, a 23 acre lake with a spring at one end where the roach used to congregate along with some tench and a few very large pike.

My father and I would go down to the Peat Pits with a casting net. I would gently push father out onto the water in a punt to the entrance of the spring hole and at the right moment he would hurl the cast net over the shoal of roach. Opening like a huge umbrella, the net would cover the shoal. Father then drew the rope tight to close the net, hauling in a few hundred roach with almost every cast. We only kept the larger fish, returning the small ones to become pike bait for another year. But there was always the chance, which we feared, that one of the monster pike down in the spring hole would accidentally be caught, probably toppling my father and the net into the pit.

The other great thing about the Peat Pits at Marshcourt was that in a hard winter the lake would freeze over and you could see the monster pike lurking below the ice. At night we would often skate on the lake by candlelight, placing straw bales round the edges to create a makeshift ice rink.

Pike were always reckoned to be the number one predator when I was a boy. One heard talk of herons and otters, but the female pike and the smaller male were thought to be worse by most riverkeepers, and we hounded these fish all through the year.

Spinning for pike during the winter months was one of our favourite pastimes; we would use a grayling or a roach mounted on a set of hooks, spinning one or the other through the water at a fairly slow pace. There is nothing like the nervous excitement you feel as you watch a roach spinning through the water, see a pike of maybe 20 lb move out from behind a clump of weed and open its large, tooth-filled jaws. At that time you could reckon on taking six to eight large pike on a winter's afternoon wherever you happened to be on the river. I wouldn't know where to find one today.

If we weren't spinning for pike in the winter we were out wiring them during the spawning months of March and April. My father and I used to go out most bright, crisp Saturdays or Sundays in the spring carrying the 18ft bamboo pole with its noose of plaited brass wire firmly attached to the end. Starting at the bottom of the Beat we moved up slowly, scanning the weed beds and slack places for fish that were either spawning or preparing to spawn.

Pike lay their eggs on weeds, usually starwort, and an obvious sign of a spawning pike is a female accompanied by two or three small attendant males. Once we had spotted this courtship 'display' we would slide the noose slowly downstream over the head of the female. She seemed quite oblivious, so once the noose was in place, my father pulled it tight and ran backwards, dropping pole, noose and pike onto the bank.

Many people ask me why we used to run backwards with the pole. It was not only because lifting the pike out of the water could break the pole but also, worse still, because of what happened to Frank Sawyer, the Upper Avon keeper. He lifted, the pike turned sharply when it felt the noose, and Frank found himself in the water.

The most prolific place for noosing pike along the whole of our stretch of the Test was Spring Ditch, a spring-fed stream running into the river at Houghton Lodge. It was an ideal place for finding spawning pike, which loved the slow-moving water where it joined the main river at the bottom of the Houghton Lodge garden. Through the years, many hundreds of pike have been taken on the wire from this little stream, but as boys we had to be careful. If Sir Lionel and Lady Wells were at home at weekends we had to refrain from chasing up and down after 'public enemy number one'. However, if we timed things right, and double-checked with the gardener, we could nip in for an hour while Sir Lionel and Lady Wells were out.

Strange as it may seem, I kept two small year-old pike as 'pets'. My father caught them for me and put them in an aquarium with some weed and a few large stones. Every day I would nip down to the river, catch some minnows and pop them into the glass box. The pike did well, in fact they did too well, outgrowing their home in a matter of months and they had to be found a new home.

What better place than the well in my friend John's garden? In those days all of the village water came either from a well or a pump. The daily feeding continued with fresh-caught minnows supplemented by the other small fish netted out of the river by the keepers, and the two pike thrived and grew.

Then John's father noticed them and the game was up.

My father came along with a long-handled net and removed them. I never quite understood why John's father was so upset, after all, he kept 'captive' pike himself, and ate them.

My other vivid memory of that aquarium is of a yellow, albino eel my father caught in the trap at Horsebridge. We kept it for ages in the aquarium on a shelf in the scullery where it seemed quite happy with its diet of worms and scraps of raw meat. However, the only problem was that on thundery nights the eel always managed to wriggle out of the aquarium and on to the floor. Instinct? You can call it what you like but I suppose the sea is where it wanted to be.

Grandfather once told me about another albino eel he caught in 1903. Over the years it grew more and more tame until it would take worms and scraps of meat from my grandfather's hand. I remember him telling me that on evenings when he was sitting in a chair near its tank, it would sometimes reach out over the edge and put its nose on the back of his neck. But in those days grandfather had a cat; the cat caught the eel and mauled it so badly it died.

My earliest recollection of fishing was sitting in a punt at the bottom of the garden at Riverside Cottage with a bamboo cane, a piece of string and no hook, wondering why I wasn't getting the instant success of other, older boys.

I soon graduated to better things when my father showed me how to catch minnows with a jam jar on a length of string. Minnows came to spawn by their thousands in Sheepbridge Shallows, so we village boys knew exactly where to sink our 1 lb jam jars, attached by a piece of string which was long enough to reach down into the water under the bridge. Minnows, particularly the males, wear beautiful spawning coats of greens, yellows and reds. These make them a highly visible target for the larger trout lurking below the shoals, which occasionally rush forward when they spot a healthy mouthful.

Poor minnows, they were so intent on doing what they had come for that nothing would put them off: neither large rushing trout nor splashing jam jars.

It was on one of these June days that I caught a specimen female minnow of 3¾in. It was a handsome fish, full of spawn and when it swam into my jam jar I thought I'd taken a gudgeon. But after a fast pull on the string, putting my hand quickly over the top of the jar, I could see it was a monster minnow. Shortly after I caught it that fish was displayed in a sample jar full of formalin in the Natural History Museum, London.

After June, when the surviving minnows had dispersed, we all changed to catching bullheads or miller's thumbs, ugly devils with rounded, flat heads and tapering bodies that could grow to 3in. in length. They lived under large stones and so, working upstream, we would carefully lift stone after stone with our left hands. If we found one at home, we quickly caught it with our right hand, paddled ashore and popped it into a can.

According to my grandfather, bullheads were gluttons for the spawn of fish, working the trout redds and gobbling up the eggs. They are also a fish you handle with care, because they have two sharp spines in the corner of their mouths. In fact, I once picked up a dead dabchick which had tried to eat a bullhead. On swallowing it had been speared by the spines, and, presumably, died of choking.

My first move into the big time with a fly rod and line was in 1933. I was seven at that time and out on the Houghton Club waters with Dr, later Sir Ivan, Magill, the famous anaesthetist who invented the Magill Tube (a rubber tube which was inserted into a patient's trachea to ensure the free passage of air to the patient's lungs during an operation). I carried Sir Ivan's bag and net and in return he allowed me to play one or two trout. My reward at lunchtime was a super box of chocolates. Sir Harold Gillies, the plastic surgeon, also took me to the river and gave me my first lessons in angling. He so impressed me on that first day I fished with him that I couldn't wait for him to come down again, hoping against hope that he would invite me to join him, which he did.

But it was my father who gave me my first proper lessons in casting the fly. One Sunday afternoon in October 1934 he took me down to the bridge at Sheepbridge Shallows for a casting lesson. At the end of the lesson he allowed me to fish a nymph downstream to a shoal of grayling and I hooked a yearling or two. I can remember that day vividly: you had to be quick with the lady of the river, and firm but not hard on the strike or, as was the case that afternoon, you'd lose more than you caught.

Back in those days you wouldn't dream of fishing your own water. After all, it belonged to the members of the Houghton Club, not the Lunn family. So that day at Sheepbridge was very much a controlled exercise. After that first day with a fly rod, my father and I regularly fished Herbert Johnson's stretch of the Test at Marshcourt, opposite the Peat Pits, where we had an open invitation.

What with fishing and earning my keep with the odd chore around neighbouring farms, life was truly idyllic for a boy growing up in a tiny village community.

Living right on the river, I learned to swim almost at the same time as I learned to run, and during the summer I was never out of the water.

I was also something of a collector, hunting butterflies in the water-meadows and moths at the river's edge. I even managed to catch a young jackdaw, raise it to adulthood and gradually teach it to speak – jackdaws are surprisingly good mimics.

One of my closest friends in those days was Luke, my father's black labrador. If ever I felt down and had nobody to play with, or my father was out fishing until late, I used to get into the kennel with Luke. In those days my father had a motorcycle and even when he was two miles from home, Luke would know he was on his way, barking long before I could hear the sound of that old bike.

Like so many boys, I also had an air gun which I would often take out in the early evenings and crouch behind a line of spears opposite the riverbank home of a water vole and practise sharpshooting as the vole scampered along the bank and took to the water. I bagged a few, but many many more dodged the flying lead.

In later, teenage years, I was introduced to more grown-up shooting in the form of shoots on Sir Eastman Bell's estate at Fosbury. They were good shots, those old boys, perhaps better than many I shoot with today.

The shoots at Fosbury were organised with meticulous, military precision, with two sets of beaters wearing white coats and the men on the sides carrying flags. Many of the Guns were Houghton Club members and included Lord Sinclair and Mr Robin Page. The undulating ground and woodlands of Fosbury lent itself to good birds. There were two sets of beaters, two guns and two loaders per shooter. One drive would come through the guns, then we'd turn round and the reverse drive would begin.

If ever the Fosbury shoot coincided with a school football match, my father always said that the shoot was more important and Sir Eastman would write to my headmaster at Andover Grammar to ensure that I got the day off. On such days I always stood next to Sir Eastman and his loader, although when the shoot was over my father and I would eat with the loaders, not the shooting gentry.

Life, however, wasn't all sunshine and freedom; looking back, it's difficult to believe how hard some things were for the villagers of Houghton and those who lived in the nearby hamlets of Bossington and North Houghton; I remember farm workers used to come down from the uplands with huge barrels mounted on horse-drawn carts and fill them with water for the livestock.

The tools my grandfather and father used were either made at home or produced by Bill Burt, the blacksmith. He was a regular jack-of-all-trades. Watching him shoe a horse is one of my clearest childhood memories. I can still see him pumping the bellows to turn the coals white hot, fashioning the horseshoes and then burning them in to the horny hooves of a carthorse the size of a mountain, knocking the nails in and filing the hooves down for a perfect fit. When I close my eyes and think of it, I can still smell that unique and wonderful odour as the hot shoe was put on to the horse's hoof.

Bill was almost a member of the family and invaluable when it came to setting the keepers' scythes. No scythe that you buy new is ever set correctly for cutting the weeds in a river, so Bill was called in to fashion the little wedges and rings and put a bend in the scythe one way or another to suit it for its job. Nowadays, setting a scythe is a welder's job: he does it just as well as Bill Burt, but I have to admit to feeling some sadness at the disappearance of the blacksmith from country life.

Harvest time was great for us village children, and the pot, because when the reaper-binder went into the field and started throwing sheaves of corn out, we were all there ready for the rabbits that would dash out of the corn. In those days, farmers cut the corn high, not close to the ground, so if a rabbit broke cover, the stubble slowed it down and we were able to hit it on the head. We would go home with up to six rabbits strung on a stick.

Needless to say, birthdays and Christmas were high points in my year. On birthdays all my friends would be invited round for tea. Probably the best birthday presents I ever received were a tricycle, which even when I outgrew it I still went on riding, though with my legs over, not under, the handlebars; my trusty Diana air gun; and my first fishing rod, which was an immaculate, if heavy, split cane fly rod.

Christmas was a big affair with the whole family gathered round the table at Riverside Cottage. As a lad there was no question about me not believing in Father Christmas; I was an only child so there was nobody to spill the beans.

On Christmas Eve I would hang a pillow case over the end of my bed. When I woke in the morning it was full of small presents: a gun with a cork in it, jigsaw puzzles, maybe ludo or snakes and ladders, always an orange or two and some nuts.

Two Christmas presents in particular stick in my mind. One was the box of chocolates I received from Sir Eastman Bell, which was the biggest box I have ever seen. It came from Swan & Edgar and must have been 1ft high and 2ft wide, with ten drawers filled with chocolates, sugar-coated brazil nuts, and ginger. I was only allowed to eat one or two on certain days of the week, but I did manage to sneak an illicit one every now and then when nobody was looking.

The other special present was given to me when I visited Shawford Park where Admiral Benson, a fishing friend of my father's lived. It was a very grand house, and when I arrived at the pre-Christmas party I felt very awkward and shy.

The Admiral, however, obviously took a shine to me, because after I had stood and admired his collection of rabbits at the back of the house, he promised to send me a couple as a Christmas present. They duly arrived, a buck and a doe, and I was given strict instructions never to put them together. Needless to say, as soon as my father's back was turned, I popped the buck in with the doe and was soon the proud owner of seven young rabbits.

I used to feed my menagerie on wild parsley and dandelion leaves. We

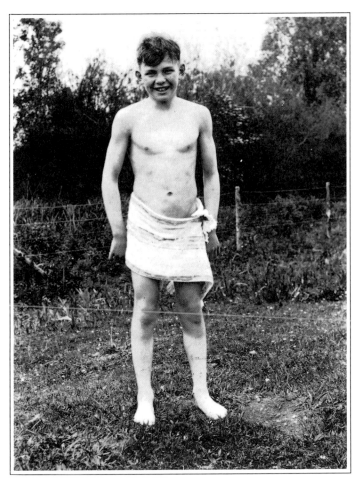

As a lad I was never out of the water during
the summer months

never ate those rabbits, they were kept simply as pets. I also used to keep fantail pigeons, which lived in a dovecote in the back garden.

Like so much else to do with my childhood, school was a constant joy. The village of Houghton and the nearby hamlets of Bossington and North Houghton produced enough children to make two classes at the village school. Miss Guy looked after the infants and Miss Hiscock taught the older children up to the age of 11. From there we went to school in Stockbridge, with the majority of children leaving school at the ages of 14 and 15 to take up jobs locally.

Luckily I passed the entrance examination and was accepted at Andover Grammar School, which meant a daily bicycle ride to Horsebridge Station where I caught the steam train to Andover.

One aspect of my education that didn't quite go according to plan was my weekly piano lesson with Mrs Cawte. There was never any doubt that I had an 'ear' for music, but I wasn't particularly quick at reading and playing the notes. However, I did have the ability to hear a tune once and play it, pretty well note-perfect. I can hear Mrs Cawte now: 'You played that beautifully, Val, but you weren't looking at the music.' I know she was most impressed, but it was obvious, and perhaps disappointing to her, that I would never read music and go on to become a famous concert pianist.

Looking back through photographs of those days at the Houghton school, I have to admit we were a scruffy-looking bunch. I was luckier than most boys because my father was quite well paid, earning about £2 a week.

Academically, too, I was lucky to have been born into a family of riverkeepers, because I was always top of the class when it came to nature studies; after all, I learned the names of the flora and fauna almost as soon as I could speak.

II

DAYS AND NIGHTS AT THE VICE

———•◦•◆•◦•———

MY grandfather died when I was 12. He had retired in 1931 as Head
Keeper of the Houghton Club waters, handing responsibility for the
river over to my father. I remember little about his working days, but I have
many memories of his retirement years; talking with him about the river and
fishing was inspiring. Even at this early age there was never any doubt in my
mind that one day I would follow in his and my father's footsteps.

Looking back fifty-six years to the time we spent together, I can now
recognise that I was in the presence of a research worker, a skilled
countryman wresting the secrets from nature. He was a patient, kindly and
gentle man; short, strongly-built and inclining to stoutness, with broad
shoulders and a deep chest. His hair was all shades of brown through to grey
and his once bright brown beard was turning white. His eyes, a clear
blue-grey, were alert and good-humoured behind his spectacles and his
speech was slow and considered, with a warm, deep resonance.

Even though he had retired, my grandfather was never far from his
beloved River Test; always on hand for advice, discussion and debate. He
also continued to encourage my father to keep a number of trout in a small
looped channel just above Riverside Cottage where the two of them would
spend many hours observing the behaviour of the fish. Many's the time I
would be sent to call them in for a meal, and there, looking down on the
channel my grandfather had dug some forty years before, would stand three
generations of Lunn: two masters of riverkeeping and a youngster eager to
learn.

Natural flies were another of grandfather's obsessions. On most days he
would spend hours studying their regeneration and determining whether

they were ovipositors, like the mayfly, or crawler downers, like all the olives except the blue winged olive. This led him to one of his most significant contributions to the art of riverkeeping: the fly board. For some while he had observed that the female olive returned to the water landing on a bridge post or a plant, crawling down into the water to lay her eggs.

What these flies did not realise when laying their eggs among the river weeds was that they were offering the many varieties of caddises a tasty meal. Bad weather apart, grandfather suspected that this predation on the eggs was responsible for those years when there were only sparse hatches of olives.

After considerable experimentation, he eventually created the fly board: one, often two, 8ft lengths of deal, designed to float below the bridges of the Houghton Club water and offer the olives a perfect landing site. The females could then crawl on to the undersides of the boards and lay their eggs well out of reach of the rapacious caddises.

Unfortunately, most of the Houghton Club's fly boards, many of them fashioned by my grandfather more than seventy years ago, have been vandalised; for some reason people think it quite a game to untie our fly boards and watch them float downstream.

I have no doubt that these boards helped to maintain the presence of the olive on the Houghton Club's 15 miles of the Middle Test, because they offered the flies a new and safe place to lay their eggs. In the future I shall try again with grandfather's fly boards, with the hope that the vandals of the Eighties will be replaced by the conservation-conscious young of the Nineties.

Grandfather also experimented with the mayfly, and his success in breeding them was a major part of the legacy he handed down to riverkeepers everywhere. As he was the first to admit, all such experiments needed a hand from nature. On still, late afternoons and evenings, the female mayfly had little trouble in making her short flight back to the water to lay her eggs. But on blustery days, the flies were weak from courtship and starvation after two days out of the water and could not raise the strength to fly into the wind to complete their lifecycle.

Mayfly are not as adaptable as the smaller ephemeroptera, or upwinged flies, like the blue winged olive, pale watery and small spurwing, which will mate and lay their eggs on a fine still morning or afternoon. The poor old mayfly will only appear in the late afternoon and early evening, when the weather is set fair and the wind is still. Grandfather always believed, and his experiments bore out his theories, that in stormy wet weather the mayfly were blown about, bruised and unable to transpose – change from dun

Grandfather taking eggs from fertilised mayflies prior to hatching
them out in the Houghton Club water

or newly-hatched fly, to spinner, the mature, sexed insect. Those that did manage to transpose were blown away from the river, and during rough stormy weather, particularly in the evenings when the male and female mayfly went through their courtship dance, the females didn't even have their final courtship fling before death.

It takes two years for the mayfly to progress from egg to nymph to dun, so if the weather is bad two years in succession and the percentage of females that manage to get back to the water is even less than the previous year, then near-extinction is on the cards. This was a situation my grandfather faced in 1906, some thirteen years after he started his experiments on restocking the river with mayfly nymphs.

In 1893, when the mayfly hatch was sparse and the weather bad, grandfather started his first experiments by collecting nymphs from the Dun, a tributary of the Test which runs in at Kimbridge, and putting them at various points in the Houghton Club waters. As a result of this restocking, the Houghton Club waters enjoyed two good seasons with the mayfly. Then came more bad weather and the fly became scarce again. In 1899 he collected more mayfly nymphs from the Kennet, but the result was just the same as it had been in 1894: a good head of fly for two or three years, then a gradual decrease until the virtual disappearance of the mayfly in 1906.

Rather than give up, grandfather hit on the idea of not only collecting nymphs, but also female mayflies. From these he gathered some 750,000 eggs on a series of glass discs and put the eggs and discs in the water, just prior to them hatching out as nymphs. Two years later the mayfly hatch was built up to its previous level, but strong winds and bad weather drove the females away from the river and the hatch was again a miserable, desultory thing.

Grandfather continued his experiments, despite the successive years of bad weather in May and June. In 1920, the million or so eggs he had put in the river two years before hatched out and the mayfly returned to the Houghton Club water in strength. Looking back through the book in the clubroom at the Grosvenor Hotel, the result of grandfather's 1918 stocking of mayfly eggs paid dividends. The hatch grew stronger and stronger in the early Twenties, peaking in 1924 with the best mayfly hatch ever recorded.

The mayfly almost disappeared from the Houghton Club waters at one other time I remember – the period between the late Fifties and late Seventies. This leads me to believe that although grandfather's experiments helped a great deal, without the aid of nature no amount of artificial breeding and restocking would have been entirely successful.

In those early years when grandfather was alive, he and my father taught me about spinning for pike with a dead fish or an artificial bait. At that time good artificial baits were hard to come by, but that didn't discourage grandfather; he made his own using the finger of a glove. He would pass a gimp – a piece of strong plaited soft wire – through the finger, then fill it with bits of grandmother's old shawl or skirt, and some lead shot. The whole concoction would then be sewn up and painted white. To give it the look of a small fish, grandfather also painted on a pair of black eyes and, with deft brushstrokes, striped the lure with green and red. A pair of small vanes were then added, to give the appearance of fins and ensure that the lure twisted enticingly through the water. Finally, a large treble hook was attached to one end and a small swivel to the other.

Grandfather's near obsession, though, was with the invention and tying of flies. This was a continuing joy for him, particularly as they were an extension of his careful, painstaking studies of the fly life of the Test.

How often I hear the cry from the more elderly anglers: 'There is nothing like the amount of fly around today, nothing like the hatches we had when I first began fishing here forty years ago.'

At this remark I pause in thought for a moment and then, without being unkind, defend my river, its appearance and condition, and suggest that their memories are not perhaps as reliable as they might be. I point out that apart from the loss of the mayfly on two occasions and the total disappearance of the grannom, which is an early season small sedge, our fly hatches have always been good, offering the trout a season-long conveyor belt of food, and rising fish for our anglers.

Certainly, the river has lost some of its condition over the years through abstraction (where the water has been taken out of the aquifers, or underground reservoirs, which feed the Test) and from agricultural chemicals and other effluent. But for me, the best indicator of the water's condition is the size and variety of the fly hatches, which are pretty well as good today as they were in grandfather and father's days.

I suppose I must have been about seven years old when grandfather introduced me to the precise art of fly tying. Once a week during the winter months my parents went to the whist drive at the Houghton village hall. On those evenings I stayed the night with my grandparents, spending much of the time sitting across the table from grandfather in the bedroom he used for tying flies. With an oil lamp between us, I would watch his large, seemingly awkward fingers create tiny flies from twists of waxed silk, fur and feather.

This small upstairs room at Riverside Cottage was grandfather's inner sanctum: his fly tying table under the window, rows of neatly-labelled boxes of feathers and fur lining the walls, his collection of nymphs and insects in bottles on the shelves. That room looked out over the woodshed to the bankside willows above Sheepbridge Shallows where I first learned to swim, where I caught my first grayling and later helped to plant the line of aspens which stand there to this day. Nobody was ever allowed into grandfather's room, except by invitation, and grandmother – who would straighten a picture that was a millimetre off-square – knew that her duster and dustpan and brush were unwelcome. The room had to be kept just as grandfather left it: nothing could be touched or tidied away.

It was there, one evening that grandfather handed me the spare vice, pliers, scissors, a few feathers and some tying silk and showed me how to

19

wind silk on a hook, choosing the largest hook he could find for me to get used to the method.

Today there are all kinds of helpful tools available to the fly tier, but then the bobbin did not exist, so the silk was tied on by hand. One refinement used by my grandfather was what he called his 'little man': a round tobacco tin filled with sand with a stick topped by a small leather washer pushed down through a hole in the centre of the tin. When the tying silk was not being used, it was trailed round the washer, which kept it well clear of the fly in the vice, leaving grandfather's hands free to set or adjust the hackle or wings.

My first ever fly, which grandmother christened Val's Own, was a simple affair with a Rhode Island Red hackle and tail and a peacock herl body. I even caught a fish with it when I was down on Marshcourt with my father, but I think that had more to do with my ability to cast accurately than the dressing of the fly deceiving the trout.

Those first hesitant steps started a passion for fly tying which has never left me. Other boys would go home from school and play with their Meccano set or jigsaw puzzle, I would spend my time with grandfather, copying his every move. In no time at all, or so it seemed, I was moving on to more difficult patterns like spinners.

In all, grandfather created forty fly patterns, four nymphs and thirty-six dry flies, with the Particular, Caperer, Houghton Ruby, Yellow Boy, Sherry Spinner, Blue Winged Olive and Orange Quill Variant among the most famous of them. In total, his fly patterns represented either the nymphs or the mature fly of almost every aquatic insect seen on or in the Middle Test, from the large dark olive of March and April to the pale watery and caperer of midsummer. To my knowledge, no member of the Houghton Club would be seen on our water without a selection of grandfather's standard patterns, carried alongside such modern favourites as the Grey and Red Wulff.

Those fly patterns, which to this day are used by flyfishers all over the world, include a number of subtle features that mark my grandfather down as the equal of such greats as Halford and Skues. Perhaps his greatest legacy to fly tying was his discovery that a stripped and dyed hackle stalk was perfect for the delicate bodies of imitative spinners and duns. This is because the touching turns of stripped hackle stalk so closely resemble the segmentation of the bodies of the natural flies, with the build-up of hackle closely representing the thorax.

These close copies of natural flies were not created by accident. They were the result of grandfather's growing knowledge of entomology and his

Thirty years of marriage – grandfather and
grandmother outside Riverside Cottage

recognition of the need for exact colours and proportions if ever an artificial
fly was to deceive the wily trout. As a consequence, grandfather was
extremely fussy when it came to the preparation of the natural component
parts of each artificial fly.

Fortunately grandmother was used to his ways and always offered each
feather or hackle stalk she dyed to grandfather for his inspection, knowing
that he might discard it because it was the wrong shade of green or yellow.
I always felt he was splitting hairs, such was his insistence on absolute
accuracy, but after hearing his complaint, grandmother would nod patiently
and dye another batch of feathers in the hope that they would be even
closer to his exact specification.

Grandmother was a lovely, small, quiet and gentle lady with a ready smile
and soft manner. She spent hours preparing grandfather's feathers, popping
them into tins with a mothball and labelling each of them according to their

use in the fly tying process. The mothball was, and still is, essential. Have you ever seen a tin of feathers after a moth grub has dined out on the contents?

She had, however, other duties as wife of the Houghton Club's Head Keeper. She also made nets with strong twine reeled around a bodkin, tying what she called her 'special knot', to ensure that the right size of mesh was created.

Nowadays dyeing feathers is a much easier affair. Back in the Thirties grandmother followed a set pattern, starting by dipping each feather in soapy water to de-grease it. If the hackle had to be a certain shade of, say, green, she would then dip it in picric acid for just enough time to re-create exactly the colour grandfather wanted. If they passed his inspection they were stored in correctly labelled boxes, like, 'hackle points: Particular', 'hackle stalks: Houghton Ruby'.

Most of the hackles used in grandfather's flies came from the poultry we kept in the back yard, which included a number of egg-laying hens and several roosters. In those days there wasn't the range of dyes that are available today, so the majority of the hackles grandfather used were of the correct natural colour. For me, that often meant a night trip with a lantern into the back of the roosting house in order to remove some vital feathers from the neck of a Blue Andalusian. Grandfather and I could then get on with tying up a few Particulars, with their natural blue necks. We also kept Plymouth Rocks for their strongly marked black and white neck feathers, Indian Game for their black feathers and White Leghorns for the purest white neck feathers. All of these roosters were quite old birds, with long spurs; grandfather always said that the older birds always gave bright, sharp strong hackles.

The home-grown roosters were not his only supply, though, because most of the local farmers knew exactly what he wanted; they never threw a dead bird away without offering it to him for inspection. He also used feathers from the annual cull of coot and moorhen, bleaching and dyeing them according to their use as part of an artificial fly pattern. If, at any time, he needed a blackbird or starling's wing, or the soft hair from behind the ear of a hare or rabbit, he would simply go out and shoot one.

His fussiness also extended to his selection of feathers; the perfect specimen for a given pattern. For example, when cutting the wings of a moorhen or coot I was instructed to cut the feathers and primaries off the wing, select the best of them and put them in labelled boxes, with the feathers from the right wing in a separate tin from those of the left. This was done so that he could select slips from each wing and tie them in so that they stood up properly, like the wings of the fly he was imitating.

I have to admit that I don't remember him buying anything, not even the ostrich herl he used for his Black Gnat pattern – that came from one of Aunty Kath's hats. He was also very quick to pull a jumper apart if he could see a colour in it suitable for tying up a specific fly pattern.

One of grandfather's fly tying tips that has stayed with me all these years, which is worth passing on to today's fly tyers, concerns the preparation of hackles. He always believed that if you stripped the hackle from the stalk to leave a nice, sharp hackle point, it should not be pulled from the stalk but cut as tight to the stalk as possible with a very fine pair of scissors. He thought that if you stripped the hackle from the stalk, it weakened it so much that there was always the chance that when winding the hackle onto the hook shank the stalk would break. This would mean starting all over again.

Grandfather was also highly inventive when it came to devising the right method for tying up his flies, and nowhere is this more evident than in his Particular. He didn't tie in the wings and then wind on the hackle stalk for the body in two separate stages. Instead he would hold the wings across the hook shank, tie in the stalks and then separate the hackle point wings with successive figure of eight turns of silk, pulling the wings in so that they were of the same length. He then folded the hackle stalks back and wound them round the hook shank, which not only gave the body of the fly a nice even look but also ensured that the wings didn't part company with the hook, no matter how many times the fly was cast.

Incidentally, grandfather always tied the hackle in first, believing that once it was tied in it was possible to judge more accurately the other proportions of the fly.

Although we were all brought up on the writings of Halford and Skues and admired their undoubted knowledge and skill, grandfather was never totally convinced that artificial flies should always so accurately mimic the natural flies they represented. So, to an extent, he broke new ground when he created a whole new series of hackled fly patterns without wings. This was because he felt that a well-tied hackle on the fly made it last longer and sit better on the water than a fly with wings did. He also reckoned that a winged fly was a devil to cast, often landing on the water and keeling over onto its side, which looked very unnatural to the trout. At a more fundamental level, which says a lot about his practical character, he believed that winged flies were produced to catch the fisherman, not the fish.

This is not to say that he ever tied a fly which was not a close copy of the originals he knew so well and studied so often. His Caperer, which has accounted for the catching of many thousands of trout on the Houghton

Club waters, is an almost exact mimic of the mature sedge of midsummer. The original is copied right down to the yellow stripe halfway down the body, which he re-created with a fibre from a swan's wing dyed yellow.

Since Halford and Skues, a lot has been written about fly design, with Brian Clarke and John Goddard going so far as to create what they call Upside Down Paraduns. This is where the dressing is tied upside down so that the hook stays clear of the water while the hackle – tied parachute-style with the hackle lying along the hook shank rather than around it – makes indentations in the surface film to mimic the fly's legs.

These patterns are jolly clever, but I often wonder whether such exactness is really necessary. After all, a large number of trout taken on the Houghton Club waters over the past ten years were deceived either by a Red or a Grey Wulff. The Wulff is a large, bushy hackled fly and bears no obvious resemblance to any living insect.

Despite all the worthy tomes written on the subject of fly fishing, I haven't yet come across one learned paper which tells us about the trout's senses of sight and smell. From my own experience of observing the trout in its natural habitat, I am convinced it has amazingly good eyesight and can tell one colour from another.

During the Second World War I remember we had to feed the trout in the stewponds with fish because horsemeat was in great demand for human consumption. Although trout thrive on eating fish, father noticed that they weren't so keen on the strips of fish he was feeding them. So he soaked the fish strips in red cochineal and then chucked them in the stewponds, and the trout went mad for them. It couldn't have been the smell which attracted them, so it must have been the colour, which more closely resembled the horsemeat we had been feeding them.

As to the trout's sight, I don't think fishermen who talk of the trout's window – meaning its angle of view – realise how large that window really is. I have more than once taken a trout by casting my fly slightly to its left or right and a little behind its head. Sure enough, it sees the fly land, opens its mouth, and turns down with the fly; if we had eyesight like that there would be far fewer muggings.

Another sense I believe fish have is that of smell. When I was young I used to go out in the shallows in July and catch the eels which were grubbing around under the stones looking for caddises. Grandfather always hated eels, believing that they were the world's worst scroungers and that they would eat almost anything, caddises, trout spawn, you name it, they gobbled it up. They were also keen on worms, so I would fix a worm on a hook, put a fairly heavy lead shot on the line and then drift the worm down to within a few feet of the eels. Sure enough, you could see the eel lift its head from the bottom, sniff the worm and then eat it.

One major thing I learned from grandfather was patience, along with nimble fingers and an ordered mind, it is the greatest gift a fly tier can have. He insisted that before starting to wind the silk on the hook, I must sort out all the raw materials in preparation for tying the flies. So I would dig out a box of ostrich or peacock herl and either strip the flue or leave it on, according to the fly pattern. Then there would be neck feathers for hackle points, stripped hackle stalks for bodies and fine fibres for the tails.

Grandfather was very particular about the materials he used and only ever tied his flies on Snecky Limerick hooks. They are the ones with the offset hook point. I don't know whether this made them better in terms of hooking the fish, but they were certainly easier to dress because the silk never fouled the hook point. He also swore by Pearsall's Gossamer silks, which were numbered according to the various shades of colour.

Of course, in those days such silk was unwaxed, so before tying up a batch of flies he and I would take our ball of wax and knead it in our hands to make it warm, soft and pliable. This wax was made by grandmother to what she called her 'special recipe', a recipe which is now unfortunately lost, as is her recipe for moorhen casserole. We then took a length of silk and waxed it thoroughly to make it nice and stiff, wound the end twice round our index fingers and started to wind it onto the hook shank. You certainly needed a very steady hand in those days; the bobbin of today makes life a lot easier.

I must have been about 10 years old when father allowed me to tie up flies for members of the Houghton Club. I remember perhaps my best earner in those days was the Black Gnat: I charged a penny for each and a shilling for a dozen.

The Black Gnat is an extremely easy fly to tie, with its stubby white wing sloping backwards, a black cock hackle and an ostrich herl body. The only really fiddly bit is tying it on a hook as small as a number 16 or number 18. On the other hand, I could tie perhaps three dozen in one evening, which brought in some extra, much-needed pocket money. Even then, father, like grandfather, wouldn't trust me to tie up a Particular: it was his special fly which required his particular skills, so to speak.

He was so precise about the making of the Particular that when a member showed him a copy of the pattern which he had bought from Hardy's shop in London and asked grandfather what he thought of its tying, grandfather turned the fly between his forefinger and thumb, thought for a moment and said, 'They've got the hook right.'

W. J. LUNN'S FLIES

Lunn's Particular
- „ Houghton Ruby
- „ Yellow Boy, Winged
- „ Yellow Boy, Hackle
- „ Sherry Spinner, Early evening
- „ Sherry Spinner, Late evening
- „ Big Orange Partridge
- „ Little Red Partridge
- „ Little Green Partridge
- „ Little Yellow Partridge
- „ Hackle Bluewing
- „ Light Hare's Hackle
- ,. Dark Hare's Hackle
- „ Hackle Caperer
- „ Gold Ribbed Upright
- „ Gilbey's Upright
- „ Black Upright
- „ Blue Upright
- „ Red Ant
- „ Dark Ant
- ,. Black Gnat
- „ Green Winged Black Gnat
- „ Nondescript Sedge
- „ Hackle Silver Sedge
- „ Hackle Red Sedge

4/- per dozen

Lunn's Winged Variants
- „ Black and Gold Variant
- „ Olive Variant
- „ Medium Light Olive Variant
- „ Blue Winged Olive Variant
- „ Orange Quill Variant
- ,. Watery Dun Variant
- „ Grey Quill Variant
- „ Ginger Quill Variant
- „ Hill's Red Quill Variant
- „ Iron Blue Variant
- „ Winged Caperer
- „ Gilbey's Little Dark Sedge
- „ Cinnanon Sedge
- „ Orange Sedge
- „ Kimbridge Sedge

5/- per dozen

Lunn's Blue Winged Olive Nymph
- „ Watery Dun Nymph
- „ Pink Nymph
- „ Greenwell's Glory Nymph
- „ Pheasant Tail Nymph
- „ Orange Partridge Nymph
- „ Olive Nymph

5/- per dozen

Alston's Favourite Hackle Mayfly
Lunn's Winged Mayfly
- „ Fibre Winged Mayfly

6/- per dozen

Lunn's Little Spent Gnat

7/- per dozen

W. J. LUNN,
2, Hill View, Rownhams Road, North Baddesley, Southampton.

Grandfather's flies – a leaflet produced after his retirement

III

LIKE FATHER, LIKE SON

I was almost six years old when my father, Alfred Walter Lunn, took over from my grandfather as Head Keeper of the Houghton Club waters in 1932. He had worked on the river since he was a teenager, became a keeper under grandfather when he was 22, and apart from four years in the Royal Flyng Corps in the First World War, his whole life was the river, its wildlife and the Houghton Club. His thirty years as Head Keeper, however, covered momentous events and changes so fundamental that they would forever affect his life, the Houghton Club and its members.

Born in 1897, he was one of four children – two boys and two girls – and it appears there was never any doubt 'young Alfred' would follow in grandfather's footsteps and become a keeper; grandmother always said that whenever father was asked what he wanted to be when he grew up he always replied, 'A fishing "gent".'

Like grandfather, he was a tireless experimenter and his contribution to the well-being of the river, its flies and the trout lives on to this day. I suppose in most ways his childhood was a lot like mine – although he had to walk the two miles across country to go to school at Broughton, whereas after junior school in Houghton and Stockbridge, I took the train to Andover and the grammar school – and, like me, his first love was the river.

I remember him being a very gentle and patient man who in looks took more after my grandmother than grandfather; I don't think he ever weighed more than 10 stone. He was also a very popular man in the village, playing billiards for the British Legion Club and football for the local village side. He also had a great sense of humour, and was forever telling new jokes he had heard from the fishing gents.

27

Mother was very house-proud and what I would call a good keeper's wife. Keepering is as hard on women as it is on men, who during the summer are out by 6am, seldom returning home until after the last member has fished the evening rise, which can often be as late as 11pm. Rather than just sit around at home, she was into everything to do with village and church life. She was a major force in the village Women's Institute and a keen member of the local amateur dramatic society and its leading player whenever it put on a comedy.

My father and I were virtually inseparable while I was growing up, and most of my knowledge of the river and its wildlife, the trout and the fly, the rod and line and the dog and gun were learned at his elbow. Walking along the river's edge, he would stop when he saw a flicker of movement in a stand of agrimony and point out the delicate colours of a tortoiseshell or red admiral butterfly; walking down North Head he would catch a fly in his hat and spend a few minutes explaining the lifecycle of the pale watery he was holding gently in his forefinger and thumb; when a fish rose some yards away from us he would explain that it was a grayling, which in rising had left tell-tale bubbles on the surface of the water.

Riverkeepers in the Thirties were a tough breed. The work was arduous and back-breaking with little or no assistance from the kind of mechanisation we enjoy now. The wages were low compared with today, but then £1 a week went much further, with beer at maybe a penny a pint and cigarettes at tuppence. Working on the river, father was also able to supplement his wage packet during the winter with the occasional otter skin fetching £3.

If grandfather came to visit the keepers at Stockbridge to oversee what they had done, he would walk almost three miles from Houghton. If their services were required by him at the Houghton end of the river they would walk downstream to Riverside Cottage. As you can imagine, there was a lot of wasted time, so to make the keepering more efficient Walter Goddard was promoted as grandfather's number one, or deputy keeper at Stockbridge, and with his crew looked after the upper end of the Houghton Club water with occasional meetings when necessary.

When I was very young, I remember father had only a solid tyre bicycle to get around on. After the roads were metalled, the members bought him a motorcycle which made his journey from Houghton to Stockbridge quicker and easier. A few years later they gave him a new Morris car, COU 95, which cost £99. It was one of the few cars in the village; I always thought it was rather grand to be driven around in it.

Around 1937 we moved from Houghton to a house in Stockbridge which we renamed 'Testlea'. This meant that father with his motor-car was able to

Father with a shoe net taking fish for restocking from the
Stockbridge stewponds

command the whole fishery, including the stewponds; it put the whole
water under one roof, so to speak.

The fish farm and stewponds at Stockbridge were created in the early
1890s; before that the Club restocked their waters with trout netted from
the various side streams lower down the Test.

The advent of better roads, faster cars and the improved rail connection
with London encouraged members to fish the water more often. As a result
father had to produce more trout and stock more liberally to supplement the
wild browns in the water, and find a sure-fire way of breeding more fish. In
so doing he revolutionised the art of hatching and rearing trout artificially,
using deep bore water instead of water from the river.

Before father's discovery, there were many theories as to why so many
trout fry died after they had absorbed their egg sacs. Some people suggested
that it might be methane gas in solution, because the Middle Test runs
through massive peat deposits; others claimed that humic acid, created by
the decomposition of plant materials, might be the killer.

As far as father was concerned, he had to find a purer source of water if he
was to successfully rear the extra trout needed by the Club. One theory he
was working on was that if he reared hatched eggs and fry in water which

came from deep below the peat, he would avoid the possibility of natural pollutants souring the water. But such a bore hole was going to cost a lot of money which could be wasted if his theory didn't work in practice. Fortunately Sir Eastman Bell, one of the Club's senior members, gave father the money to prove his point.

Work started in 1953 and I watched in wonderment as the water diviner was summoned and duly arrived complete with hazel twig in each hand. After a few quiet words with father he started to walk slowly around the paddock, his twigs twitching furiously as he methodically covered every square foot of land. It must have been quite a strange sight to anyone watching: my father and I standing to one side while this raggedy-looking man, his long hair and beard almost merging, walked intently around the paddock staring at the two madly gyrating twigs he was carrying. Eventually he settled on one spot, pointed to the ground and said, simply: ' 'Tis deep, but very strong.'

We set to work with a drill and over several days we bored deeper and deeper until at 110ft a steady trickle of clear water began to run out of the top of the hole. Before embarking on building a new hatchery, father put a zinc bath over the bore hole and put a handful of trout fry in it. The following morning he and I went down to see how the fry were getting on, only to find that they had all disappeared. We scratched our heads and rather foolishly looked around to see if they had somehow grown wings. But the wings belonged to the kingfisher which fluttered across and perched on the side of the bath, presumably thinking we were about to feed him again.

We covered the bath with a fine mesh netting and repeated the experiment to find that the fry thrived on the clear spring water, which unlike the river water was not contaminated by pollutants and ran at a constant 50°F.

Father duly built the new hatchery, designing it to hold up to 750,000 trout ova. The following year his theory became fact when we lost only 20 per cent of the 28-day-old fry, as opposed to something like 95 per cent in previous years. This obviously offered father more yearlings to choose from so that he could select only the finest for growing on to their second year when they would be put in the river. It also enabled him to net out several hundred three-month-old trout and put them in the river to supplement the native wild trout population; it is a practice we have continued to this day. The new bore hole hatchery was also the birthplace of the Houghton Club's commercial fish farming operation, which today makes a substantial contribution to the Club's finances.

Over the next five years, through rigorous selection of only the finest trout, he was able to take all the fish he wanted from a brood stock of 2 lb 8 oz to 4 lb trout whereas before he had taken eggs from fish of under 2 lb. I have continued his work over the years and I am now breeding more, bigger, and better fish from the selective breeding methods he instituted.

Not that it was all plain sailing. Father had to constantly keep an eye open for losses of the mature fish in the stewponds through disease. In his day, the two main killers were saprolignia – a fungus that mostly affected the male trout after spawning and was only controllable after the introduction of Malachite Green; and furunculosis, a stress disease affecting fish after spawning or during warm weather when the water temperature rose in the summer months. The only way to cure furunculosis was to mix sulpha-methazane with the trout's food. Since then, better drugs have come along and today I use aqualinic acid.

But there were other problems which were not quite so easy to remedy, like the year the water authority – in those days known as the Catchment Board – embarked on a scheme which threatened the future of the River Test. Mr Macdonald, the Board's resident engineer, was mad keen on land drainage as a way of preventing flooding, and as far as he was concerned the only solution was to dredge the river, remove the weirs and get the whole lot into the sea as quickly as possible.

In 1942 he started work at the bottom end of the river, dredging out the bed with drag lines and removing weirs as he worked his way upstream. Recognising the considerable long-term harm this would do to the river, my father contacted a high-powered team of like-minded experts and the battle began. It took several months, with the Board getting closer and closer to the Houghton Club's water, but commonsense eventually prevailed and work was stopped. As my father explained at the time: nobody wants the land to flood, but water is too important a commodity to simply rush it down to the open sea. The more practical solution to the danger of flooding was to have good controls which would give keepers up and down the valley the ability to adjust the height of the water; opening the hatchways in high water times and closing them down in low water months.

Father was right, of course, and today a few miles downstream the scars of that dredging work are still visible, with the Test running between high banks: it was certainly no way to treat a chalkstream. The work done by succeeding authorities on our river has been varied: they have done some good, building new weirs and controls and revetting the banks where necessary. Fish passes and counters have also been installed with the co-operation of fishery owners up and down the Test Valley in an effort to find out how many salmon are making it upstream to spawn, but at present I am sceptical about whether these constructions are ultimately going to tell us anything new.

Although many of father's experiments were highly successful, some were failures. One that seemed like a good idea misfired quite badly: he thought he'd try feeding trout alevins and fry on nymphs of the reed smut and the fry loved these tasty morsels, but the alevins got caught up and died in the webs that the reed smuts had woven.

Father was a tireless student of nature and one of his many discoveries was that *Dytiscus marginalis* (the great diving beetle) was capable of tearing with its formidable pincers and eating fry which were placed in a nursery lacking a sufficient flow of water. When he increased the water flow in the nursery the beetles flew off elsewhere for a fish supper: his discovery saved quite a number of trout fry.

Father always told me that his three major concerns were fish, fly and river management. When it came to fly on the Middle Test he, like grandfather, attempted to restock our waters with fly, in particular the grannom, and made improvements to the original fly boards to make the most of every fall of spinners and keep them on our own stretch of river. For some years he had noticed that many spinners failed to alight on the original fly boards because there was nothing for them to hit against. By adding wooden shields at intervals along the boards he found that the spinners hit the shields, landed on the boards and crawled beneath them to lay their eggs.

The Houghton Club had been without the grannom for several years when father bought eggs from Nursling, lower down the river, in 1938. Some of the eggs were put into the river in perforated crates while the rest were brought on fly boards which were put in the river at the Mill and Picket Mead Weir. Those on the fly boards hatched out well, but those in the crates did not have a sufficient flow of water and few hatched out. The experiment was a short-lived success, however, with a few trout taken on the artificial grannom the following year. It is sad to say that since those days the grannom has become extinct on the Middle Test; on the Lower Test, where they cut less weed, the grannom continues to flourish.

The brief reappearance of the grannom was, however, overshadowed that autumn when Britain declared war on Nazi Germany. By then I was 13 and studying at Andover Grammar School, but I well remember those days when all the young keepers went off to war to be replaced by a couple of pensioners, long retired from riverkeeping, who included my 65 year-old grandfather on my mother's side. The Club committee also decided to sell off a number of trout to the Army Catering Corps in an effort to save money

Father changing a fly at Bossington Hatches, 1960

on fish food. Within a year this proved a wise move as horseflesh became harder and harder to get.

Father tried a number of alternatives, including powdered hard-boiled eggs cooked for 20 minutes and fed dry to the fry in the nursery. He also tried finely minced raw liver, which worked well but was very time-consuming and messy. Father was always looking for an alternative, but it wasn't until I had been Head Keeper for a few years that modern pelleted feeds came along and made our lives considerably easier.

In addition to attempting to maintain the quality of fishing on the Houghton Club waters – with few members coming down, rods were offered to a number of officers based in and around Stockbridge – father was also asked to oversee the war work on the river to ensure that no lasting damage was done.

At the beginning of the war it was decided to make the river a line of defence in case the Germans invaded and a number of pillboxes were built. However, the idea lost favour when someone pointed out that if the Germans did invade, their tanks could easily cross the river at any one of the many shallows. Sheepbridge Shallows, however, was pressed into service when a section of it was dredged and two concrete ramps were built to simulate the ramps of a tank landing craft. It was here that the army tested their vehicles, from jeeps to three ton trucks, to make sure their engines were adequately waterproofed. We still call that part of the river the 'Tank Trap' and one or two of the concrete bases of the pillboxes have been used to erect fishing huts.

By this time father had gone back into uniform, first as captain and second-in-command of D Company, 1st Battalion Hampshire Home Guard, and in 1943 as its major and commanding officer. The year before he had led the march of the Home Guard's Stockbridge platoon at the Stockbridge and District Warship Week parade with the Third Sea Lord, Admiral Sir Bruce Fraser, taking the salute outside the Grosvenor Hotel.

As must have been the case with every town, village and hamlet in those tough war years, everyone tried to live as normal a life as possible, with the same round of fêtes, parties and dances. Father was responsible for organising dances most Saturday nights in the Stockbridge Town Hall. It was always a full house and the girls from the surrounding villages flocked to Stockbridge at weekends, knowing that the Hall would be full of young soldiers.

On one particular Saturday the band father had booked couldn't make it through the heavy snow which cut the town off from the outside world. By now I had left Andover Grammar School and was working for my father, often doing the heavier jobs to help out the pensioners he had as under keepers during the war. On that winter night, however, I may well have become something other than a riverkeeper, because I was called in to see if I could rustle up some music so as not to disappoint the waiting dancers.

I immediately got hold of Jack Parker, who played the clarinet. Then there was Dave Sparks on double bass or fiddle, John Hurst on trumpet, Maurice Rideout on drums and me on piano. The people there must have enjoyed it because after the whip round they gave us £2 each, which was a fortune in those days. As we were packing up after the dance, a sergeant from Wallop camp came over and said he wanted to book our quintet for one

Me at Sheepbridge Shallows

The top of Asham's Arm on the Machine Beat, the bank coloured
by clumps of purple loosestrife and yellow fleabane

of the camp dances, and the Dots and Dashes (named after the Morse code we had been learning in the Air Training Corps) was formed.

After a few nights' rehearsals we listed a load of dance tunes – waltzes, foxtrots, quicksteps and the like – and blow me if we didn't start to get bookings, first at the nearby army camps and then for all sorts of functions. None of us had a car so we used to load all our instruments and ourselves into Charlie Harfield's taxi. As people got to know us better we found ourselves working four nights a week, sometimes doing a fête in the afternoon and a dance in the evening. We used to charge something like £1 each a night, which meant that in 1942 I was probably earning more than my father. We added more musicians to the band, including a chap called Ron Marquis, who was a fireman on the Great Western Railway; he went on to play saxophone in Cyril Stapleton's dance band.

In November 1944, though, my musical career and any hope of being another Henry Hall or Cyril Stapleton went by the board when I was called up and eventually joined the Devonshire Regiment. I received my commission in 1946 and served as a lieutenant with the Devonshires in the Far East until I was demobbed on New Year's Day 1948.

The Second World War was grim for everyone, but for father it did have its lighter side. Among the many officers who took up the offer to fish the Houghton Club waters was General Beddell Smith, General Eisenhower's Chief of Staff, who was headquartered near Portsmouth. He was no slouch with a fishing rod and on about four visits caught quite a few trout. He was obviously thrilled to be able to take time off from the war in Europe and asked if he could bring Ike over to Stockbridge with him. Father and I fished with them, and although they spent several hours in the hut on North Head – father believed they must have been discussing the campaign in Europe following the invasion – they enjoyed a classic Houghton Club evening rise. They must have had a good time because a week or so after they had been down father was asked by Beddell Smith if he would like to fly over to France and see how things were progressing. The only stipulation was that father wore his Home Guard uniform.

Father readily accepted the invitation and early one morning a chauffeur-driven camouflaged limousine arrived at the door of Testlea to take him on the first leg of his journey. I remember mother was quite tearful when she waved father goodbye, pleading with him to be careful. He was, and after two days returned loaded down with wine and Camembert cheese. With a huge smile he recounted how he had overheard one of our soldiers say to another: 'Things must be bad, mate, they've called in the Home Guard.'

Although rationing continued into the Fifties, life returned to normal after the war. But a river is a problematic thing at times and father was soon faced with yet another dilemma. This time it was pike; in 1949 the water was infested with them.

It's not easy to understand why a river suddenly becomes full of pike. Grandfather always reckoned it had something to do with the weather, insisting that the severe cold in the early months of the year meant that the pike escaped capture. He had experienced the same sudden explosion in the pike population in the 1890s and according to my father always said that it was likely to happen again.

In grandfather's day it took ten years to get the pike population under control, but with this sudden resurgence in 1949 – when my father caught several hundred in pike traps laid down throughout our waters – he managed to persuade the Club to invest in an electric fisher, which passes a small charge of electricity through the water, stunning all fish within a few yards. The next year he electro-fished the Houghton Club waters and removed 365 fish, one for every day of the year. Since then we have electro-fished the water most years and the pike have never returned in any great numbers.

The post-war years also saw the revival of fly rod technology. The split cane rod, which very quickly took the place of the original whipping rod, was heavy and was only available in a limited variation of actions. Recognising this, several companies experimented with different materials for producing fly rods that offered a series of different actions for different kinds of flyfishing. One such company was Babcock and Wilcox, who deluged father with steel blanks for him to test. He eventually found one that worked well, but the fad only lasted a few months until the first glass fibre rod was manufactured. Since then, manufacturers on both sides of the Atlantic have produced ranges of carbon fibre and boron fly rods which are lighter and stronger and which offer as many actions as there are fly fishermen.

At this time father was in great demand as a consultant, advising a number of owners whose waters in Hampshire and Wiltshire had been neglected during the war years. In 1949 he was also called in by the Driffield Angling Club in Yorkshire who were looking to improve the Driffield Beck after many years of neglect. What was needed was for father to cast his skilled and experienced eye over the water so he could draw up a detailed plan aimed at returning it to its former glory. This he did and on one of his trips north he took me with him; it was, he said, all part of my education.

On that trip I met Sir Robert Ferens who was the driving force behind the

Outside the Grosvenor Hotel at the start of a day's play –
(from left) myself, Sir Laurence Dunne and father, 1963

scheme. Father's plans were agreed and two hard-working chaps were set to work under the direction of a keeper that father had found for the club. Gradually, over a number of months, the water was reborn and is to this day regarded as the equal of any southern chalkstream.

Many years later, after father had died, I travelled back to the Driffield Beck with the President of the Houghton Club to celebrate the Driffield Angling Club's 150th anniversary. It was a splendid occasion and in his speech at the dinner, Sir Robert Ferens praised Alfred Lunn for the effort and interest he had given to what is now a thriving angling club. Sir Robert also presented the Houghton Club with a handsome ceramic kingfisher under a glass dome as a memento of the occasion. It carries the inscription: 'Presented to the Houghton Club by the Driffield Anglers in appreciation of their generous help in 1949.'

In the fifties father was approached by Sir Eric Savill, a club member who was also the Chief Ranger and creator of the Savill Gardens at Windsor Castle. He asked if father would take a look at a loop of the River Thames where it ran through the grounds below the Castle. Sir Eric thought it might make a good little trout fishery, so father and I went along for a reconnaissance. Although it would never be like our own River Test, the water quality was acceptable and father produced a report suggesting a grid at either end to keep out some of the coarse fish – such as pike and perch. He also advocated electric fishing to get the rest of the coarse fish out in readiness for stocking the water with trout.

His plan was accepted and we duly arrived to take out the coarse fish, which included pike, perch, rudd, roach, in fact just about every known coarse fish in addition to quite a number of eels. During the course of electro-fishing the water we were joined by the Royal family. Prince Charles, who was then a young boy, joined us in the boat and seemed to thoroughly enjoy helping us net the electrically stunned fish, getting very muddy into the bargain, while Her Majesty the Queen stood on the bank, taking photographs of the unlikely scene.

At the end of the day we returned all the coarse fish to the Thames outside our fenced-off section. Later we stocked the newly cleared stream with trout in the hopes that those entitled to fish it would find time to do so.

The rainbow trout was another of the challenges which faced father during his years as Head Keeper. He had known for many years that the American rainbow was a splendid import to this country and although he agreed with Frederic Halford – who described the rainbow as 'a grand fighter' that 'grows rapidly to a great weight' – he didn't agree with him that it had cannibalistic tendencies and had a 'propensity to work down the river. . . .' and 'should be classified among the migratory, or anadromous, species of the Salmonidae'.

The members of the Houghton Club, however, were split over whether father sould stock the rainbow. Some of them agreed with Halford, others agreed with my father and like-minded authorities who could see the advantages of breeding fish that grew more rapidly and fought harder than brown trout.

In 1949, after much soul-searching and debate the Club agreed to allow my father to stock the water with the shasta rainbow, which today continues to be the pure strain of American trout in the Club's waters.

As you can imagine, my father built up quite a reputation over the years he was Head Keeper of the Houghton Club and it is largely due to his pre-eminence as a riverkeeper that I am in demand to advise fisheries on the

Test and the Itchen, as well as supply them with brown and rainbow trout.

I would think that every son has a problem writing about his father, with his views mixed up in a cocktail of emotion and commonsense. I knew my father to be a gentle, patient and clever man, who worked tirelessly to produce the best fish and fishing in the Test Valley and in so doing generously offered his considerable knowledge to those who needed it.

Barrie Welham, a Lunn family friend for many, many years, summed up my father's career in June 1970 when he wrote, upon father's death in April of that year:

> Alf Lunn had few equals. His ability to spot, and pinpoint, the rise of a good fish, plus his quick and positive identification of fly, both in the air and on the water, added much to the enjoyment of whoever he was with.
>
> Those of us who know the river, which he did so much to maintain and improve, will greatly miss his trim, spry figure. I think he enjoyed every one of his 72 years, for his lifetime coincided with the very peak of the dry fly fishing cult. With modern agricultural sprays, road washings and insecticides, it can never be as good again. It is almost as if the death of Alfred Lunn is indeed the passing of an era.

IV

A RIVERKEEPER'S YEAR

———◆———

Stockbridge is the most famous of the world's fisheries: on its lovely succession of deeps and shallows, racing rapids and swinging stretches, all as though arranged to give the dry fly man every variety of shot.
John Waller Hills, *A Summer on the Test*, 1924

THE art of keeping a river has changed little since my grandfather's day. That's because work on any river is seasonal, it's only the tools we use that have changed, and in many ways made the riverkeeper's life an easier one.

However, it's the work a keeper does or doesn't do in what's called the 'close' season – from 1 October to 31 March – that will either make or mar the following season's sport; a fact which has prevailed for more than 160 years on the Houghton Club's 15 miles of the Middle Test.

Most people expect me to heave a great sigh of relief when the last member has packed his rods and had his last whisky and soda of the season in the clubroom at the Grosvenor Hotel. After all, come 1 October we have been at full stretch for six months with the river, fish and fishermen.

It is a time of nostalgia for me, an abrupt ending to days on the river with members and their guests. It is when I remember the moments of triumph, the missed opportunities and the evenings of companionship, conversation and debate in the clubroom. Come 1 October, however, the clubroom is cocooned for another season, the book is totalled up and put away in its cabinet, and dust begins to settle on the oak dining table.

Workwise, of course, the year is really just beginning for a riverkeeper. More often than not, October is the month of the lowest and clearest water, which makes the job of electric fishing and netting considerably easier. In October, we are able to be much more effective with the electric fisher, especially in the middle and lower reaches where the Test runs deeper. Electric fishing for pike in the upper reaches, where the water is not so deep, can be a pre-spawning, springtime operation.

In grandfather's day, they used to take anything up to 900 pike in the autumn and spring using spinners, roach live bait and the brass wire noose. However, following the advent of the electric fisher in my father's day, the pike population has been reduced to about a dozen each season.

A lot of people ask me if electric fishing is dangerous. After all, like oil and water, electricity and water don't mix. I have never experienced any electric shocks, only 'tickles', but we have more than once gone down with all hands. Picture the scene: there are four of us in midstream in the punt with several bins of grayling and pike on board. Someone shouts, 'There's a pike on the right hand side, just under that weed,' and we all peer over the side. The boat tips and lets in water and we find ourselves gradually sinking, finishing up with four of us standing up in a boat that is 4ft under water.

For us, the main jobs during the autumn and winter every year are trimming the bankside vegetation and weed cutting. The former gets rid of all the old herbage so that new, fresh growth can come through in the following spring, and it gives us a chance to cut away any encroaching roots which are making their way out into the stream.

The autumn weed cut is designed to dispose of a good deal of the weed which has grown furiously since the last cut in August. By cutting it we are able to ensure that through the winter the river-bed doesn't fill up with mud and silt. Much of our time is taken up with the river weed which lies close to the banks, particularly those large patches on the idle corners of the river that, if left, could choke the flow and in time become solid mud banks.

Keepers down the ages have always said, 'Look after the sides and the middle will look after itself,' an old adage which rings true today. Mind you, with 15 miles of river and carriers – which are the side streams of the main river – to care for, the autumn weed cut can take us until February to complete.

Maintaining a tidy, well-kept river is only one aspect of the first few months of the close season, it is a chore which has to go hand-in-hand with attending to the fish farm and breeding trout of a quality and size that complement one of the most beautiful and famous stretches of the Middle Test.

The first job in the fish farm is to drain down the stewponds – the narrow

Netting fish out of the stewponds in Stockbridge prior to grading the trout
for the coming season

trenches fed by river water where we raise our trout – and purge them of any
lurking bugs and growths with a sprinkling of lime. It's a messy but
necessary job, one which ensures that when the stewponds are re-filled and
stocked with growing trout, their home is clear of any possible problems
which could affect their well-being and growth. Hygiene is always upper-
most in the fish farmer's mind. At the same time, we are grading or selecting
the best of the trout as brood stock for the hatchery.

Grading involves splitting the fish up according to their size. Of the
20,000 yearlings in our stewponds some are 3in. long, others 10in. long,
despite the fact that they are all the same age. Our first grading separates
the larger fish from the smaller ones because these faster-growing trout are
the bullies, the pushers who have dominated the feed hoppers.

Once you get them into their new homes, the smaller fish make better
progress and you end up with a more even growth rate across the 20,000
fish. You will always have some which do better and these will be selected,
particularly from July onwards, as spawning stock. We even go to the

42

trouble of selecting those fish with particularly bright red spots, hoping that the colouration will come through in their progeny. Generally speaking, our spawning stock comprises about 80 hens – which will weigh between 5 lb and 8 lb – and 30 cock fish.

Come the third week in November, the females are ready for spawning and the hatchery has been made ready to accept the first batch of ova stripped from our pregnant female brood stock.

A lot of the work that goes into the hatchery involves checking and cleaning out the pumps that supply it with fresh spring water; the hatching troughs, too, are all cleaned and repainted. The qualities of spring water mean that the trout eggs hatch after only 40 days incubation. On river water it can take anything from 80 to 100 days, depending on the water temperature; the sediment in the river water is yet another problem.

In short, spring water has made rearing fish an easier and surer business. The only drawback is that spring water lacks oxygen. However, this can be put right if the water is plunged into the holding tanks, then 'fizzed' through taps into the hatchery, so that it picks up oxygen from the air.

The first stripping of the Houghton Club brood stock takes place in mid-November and we expect to gather around 100,000 ova. If all runs smoothly, it is completed in a morning. This gives us the afternoon to treat the whole brood stock, spawned and unspawned, with a fungicide; an essential process after all the handling the fish have received.

A second spawning takes place about fourteen days later, and we collect as many extra ova as we feel are required. The remaining females are also stripped out, mostly because I believe it's better to help the female trout over what is a stressful time for them, and get them back on the road to recovery before the coldest of the winter weather sets in.

In the hatchery, the keeper in charge cleans the grids or screens, keeps an eagle eye on the stock and feeds the fish daily. He watches over the eggs, disinfecting them regularly until the alevins, or young fish, arrive.

The methods we now use during spawning are very different from those employed by my grandfather and father. In grandfather's day it was reckoned that there were two reasons why natural wild trout spawning was not too successful. One reason was thought to be the high level of methane in the water. The other reason was the silt which seemed to settle in the shallows and clog up the trout redds – the areas in the shallows where the trout buried their fertilised ova – preventing the swift flow of oxygenated water over the eggs.

My grandfather thought up a way to get round this problem, and that was to dig or plough over the shallows before spawning took place to dislodge

Keeper Ron Dumper filling the automatic feeders at the
Stockbridge hatchery

the silt. I have to admit, the trout seemed to prefer these ploughed over areas and the results were encouraging in terms of the increase in wild stock. But it wasn't the whole answer.

Even after father discovered that the ova thrived on spring water drawn from below the peat, the keepers still walked the carriers in search of spawning fish. Once found, they were collected and brought back to the hatchery in fish kettles where they were stripped and the ova put in the spring-fed hatchery; until the advent of pelleted foods, the ova from trout reared on horseflesh were unusable.

With the early November spawning and hatchery work over, the only other important collective job for the keepers is the weekly dipping of our mature trout in Malachite Green. It's a horrid job because one morning every week between 1 November and 1 May, whatever the weather, we net up all the fish in each stewpond, seal off the water intake and add the correct amount of fungicide for about two minutes. If this job is carried out as described, we know we are guaranteed a healthy stock of fish for the coming season. I have always worked on the principle that prevention is significantly better than cure; it's so much better to stop trouble happening than it is to try and put it to rights.

Before the use of fungicides, my father accepted something like a 15–20 per cent mortality rate in his mature fish stocks. Obviously, some years were kinder than others, but as a teenager I remember how upset my father was when he had to throw hundreds of mature, beautifully-marked trout – which he had brought on from alevins, fed daily and nurtured to muscular, mature fish – into a lime pit for disposal.

Although fungicides and antibiotics are a positive sign of progress, extra vigilance is also necessary in these modern times. The dramatic increase in the number of fish farms up and down the Test Valley with high stocking rates has, in my view, introduced a whole series of bugs that didn't exist in my father's day.

Fishermen often say to me that I'm lucky to be upstream from the fish farms in the Test Valley. Maybe so, but when bugs get into a river system they get to you eventually, whether you are up or downstream. I really don't believe this lovely river was made to be over-burdened with millions of small, scruffy 'table' trout.

Come the second half of November, with the majority of the collective tasks completed in the stewponds and hatchery, I tend to split the keepers into two teams: three river trimmers to continue with the weed cut and bankside clean-up, and two keepers to begin on the river carpentry.

In grandfather and father's time there was an estate carpenter. Today we have a first-class man: a keeper, carpenter, mechanic, a you-name-it-he'll-do-it man who is vital to the running of a fishing estate the size of the Houghton Club. Most of my under-keepers will do their own carpentry on the sections of river under their care. They make do and mend things like seats, bridges, fences and bank revetting; but when renewal rather than repair is necessary, our jack-of-all-trades is called in.

Because of the length of our fishery, I find it best for the keepers of each Beat to draw up a list of jobs. This allows the carpenter to complete them systematically.

December is a busy time. In the week before Christmas the ova start to hatch. It is just 35 days since the rainbow trout eggs were laid and 42 days since the brown trout eggs were laid.

Besides giving satisfactory hatching conditions, spring water is also ideal for bringing the small fry on to the feed, and keeping them on it for the first three months. I usually move our young fish to river water in March, when the temperatures of the springs and the river coincide. However, the move isn't a one-step operation. I prefer to keep young trout on a mixture of river and spring water for two to three weeks so that they acclimatise gradually.

Tending young trout is a relatively simple business, but strict rules have to be followed if we are to make the most of the ova we stripped two months before. Here, again, my rule of prevention being better than cure comes into play, because I make sure that all the young are subjected to a weekly bath of disinfectant to keep them in good order. This treatment has put paid to the age-old problems of Bacterial Gill Disease and fungal bloom. We are also careful not to overcrowd our new fish stocks in the hatchery; overcrowding can cause problems for fish, as it can for all animals.

Soon it's New Year. It seems an age since September when I saw the last trout caught and now we're heading for the worst time of the year, January and February, when the weather can have an appalling effect on all the work we have yet to do before spring arrives.

Winters like the one spanning 1962 and 1963, which was the year I took over from my father as Head Keeper, are not welcome to people like us who have to work outside all day. It was one hell of an introduction to my new job, because that particular year we had snow on the ground before Christmas and that same snow was still there in March. There were prolonged freezing temperatures by day and night and the ponds in the fish farm were frozen over. Even the spray from the inflows at the top of each of the stewponds froze, and the screens were blocked with ice. It's the first time I've ever experienced such long periods of freezing weather, a time when the river water temperature was at freezing point and cotton-woolly ice hung from the weeds. For the first time in perhaps fifty years, the water-meadows flooded because the hatchways had iced up.

I've never been so cold as I was that winter. I seemed to spend hours every day clearing ice from the screens in the fish farm so that the water could flow out of the stews, despite the thick ice-caps covering them.

Fortunately, trout feed less often in such ice-cold conditions and it wasn't necessary to handle them to check for diseases because there were fewer diseases around. But even though we restricted feeding them to once a week, we still had to break a hole in the ice and drop the minced horseflesh in; pellets hadn't been invented twenty years ago. The rest of our time was spent de-icing the weirs on the river with sledgehammers and crow-bars.

Everything we did that winter was cold and miserable but the thaw came, eventually. Looking back through the book in the clubroom at the Grosvenor Hotel, I can see it was all worth it because the Houghton Club members and their guests had a good season. In the book for that year

Riverkeeping has changed little since grandfather's day, particularly when it comes to stocking the river

Commander Vivian Robinson, the Club's secretary, wrote:

> Despite the cold winter and wet summer, the fishing was excellent. Mick Lunn is to be congratulated for his work in this, his first year as Head Keeper.

Luckily, the winters since then have been mostly mild, which suits the keepers and the fish.

Apart from the weather, which as a riverkeeper has affected every day of my life for the past twenty-eight years, the other problem confronting and concerning me on a daily basis is the possibility of disease.

Our greatest scourge was the arrival of UDN, or Ulcerative Dermal Necrosis, in the winter 1967–8. Fish affected by UDN develop an ulcer on their noses which then grows a fungus, or saprolignia. This spreads very rapidly and the fish die very quickly. Apart from the speed with which it can kill, it is also highly contagious, spreading from a contaminated fish to all trout that come into contact with it.

I first saw trout affected by UDN in a stewpond five miles downstream. At the time I didn't know what the disease was, so I told the owner to kill all the fish right away, which he did. It seemed wrong to take a chance, the risk was too great, particularly as there were only three hundred fish in the pond. His trout had come from a fish farm on a watercourse which had some reports, albeit vague, of being affected by this new disease. Few of us knew anything about it, even though some Scottish salmon rivers had been reporting losses through the disease. Back on our waters, though, there was no sign of this mystery killer and our season started off well.

In the autumn I was invited back to the same stewpond below the Houghton Club waters and was aghast to find that the fish had been stocked from the same source and were affected by the same disease, which I took to be UDN. Unfortunately, the tell-tale ulcers had not been spotted immediately and when I arrived I noticed that in the outflow from the stewpond into the main river the trout had ulcerated heads.

Luckly, my fish were 5 miles upstream so I felt there was perhaps time to do something. My biggest fear was that the migratory salmon, which were on their way up river to spawn, would become infected and bring the disease with them to the Houghton Club.

On my return to Stockbridge I acted quickly. First I called my friend Ivor Noble, a farmer who had a large spring-fed lake at the top of a watercress farm in nearby Sherfield English. Recognising the emergency, he agreed to play host to two thousand of my mature brown trout which we ferried over to his lake, four hundred at a time, by tractors and trailers.

They immediately took to their new home, and Ivor the farmer became Ivor the Houghton Club's acting, unpaid keeper with instructions to keep his eyes peeled for herons and poachers and give his new livestock three buckets of protein pellets a day.

Although I popped over to the farm twice a week to see the fish and give Ivor encouragement, there was little need. He watched over them like a guardian angel.

With the mature brownies well taken care of, I turned my attention to the trout already in our stretch of the river. My first job was to deter any UDN-affected salmon spreading the disease through our waters. I placed two electrodes in the open hatchways of a weir on the main river side of the valley which I knew that salmon moving upstream would have to pass through. This hastily-rigged system ran day and night for six weeks, during which time quite a few salmon were moving upstream to spawn. My electric shock treatment certainly worked, because during the run I witnessed a number of fish feel the tickle of volts and amps and quickly disappear downstream from whence they came.

My final measure was to ensure that the remaining trout in the stewponds were dipped twice weekly in a fairly concentrated soup of Malachite Green. This was because I was working on the principle that the ulcer may not be the killer, but the secondary invader, the fungus, surely was. Not very scientific, I'll admit, but it was better than sitting on my hands and doing nothing.

From Christmas 1967 until mid-May 1968, the Test gave up a lot of its fish because of the new disease, with the wild brownies and salmon suffering most. In our own stewponds we killed off quite a few trout that were beyond recovery but generally speaking the dipping worked wonderfully. We had little or no fungus, and the ulcers eventually healed over by May and, we hoped, the mended fish had achieved some immunity to the disease.

Happily, the fish we had moved to Ivor's lake showed absolutely no sign of any disease and in late May we ferried them the 20 miles back to our own waters. These were the fish which contributed considerably to the good sport of the members and their guests throughout the next season on the River Test.

As a consequence of that initial scare, between 1969 and 1974, I kept slightly more rainbow trout than brownies, simply because the rainbows were unaffected by UDN.

Since that first year, UDN has gradually subsided and now, more than twenty years later, we are still employing preventative treatments in the fish farm. Although this obviously creates extra work, it seems to be worth it. Other keepers up and down the Test Valley are certainly grateful for our extra effort since most of their stretches of water are stocked with fish reared in the Houghton Club farm.

Fortunately, our swift action and regular treatment of the Houghton Club trout meant that our members and their guests were ignorant of the problems we and the river were going through. But after all, we were only doing our job.

In the days of top hats, a wind was necessary in order to lift the blowline. So trees near the river were either cut or lopped, exposing the waters to all the wild airs which sweep that lively valley.

John Waller Hills, *River Keeper*, 1934

WHATEVER the weather, mid-January is a time for checking the river-bank.

Unlike the northern and western rain-fed rivers – which annually burst their banks – our chalkstreams seldom flood. Which is not to say that we don't lose water through holes and breaches. It's for this reason that I always spend time walking the full length of the Houghton Club waters, noting down areas of bank which need mending or repairing. On these walks I'm looking for places where water is weeping or leaching through the bank. Such small leaks can become major breaches; cattle and water-voles have a lot to answer for here.

In grandfather's time such breaches were repaired with faggots made from bundles of sticks and twigs bound tightly together and filled with chalk. They were then revetted front and back.

Moving into February, the shortest month of the year, we finish off trimming the banks and grab off and scoop out any corners which have silted up. Sometimes we create temporary groynes to help us shift the unwanted mud which can interfere with the free flow of the stream.

In grandfather and father's time they used mud pans, hauling tons of mud and silt onto the banks. It's a tradition that has not survived, because it was a time-consuming and labour-intensive method as well as being very hard work.

Now, the modern keeper believes in sending his rubbish downstream to another's water, with the 'I am all right, Jack' attitude. He will grab the silt away and site groynes to force the river current through his mud bank, or use a machine if access is possible.

On the Houghton Club water, however, we are more careful with our weed cutting during the summer. As a result, the mud and silt can be stopped from filling the idle corners of the river. For example, if weed is left to grow opposite a bad corner, then the flow will be diverted and mud and silt will not settle there.

At the end of February and the beginning of March we turn our attention to the trees lining the bank. We start with pollarding the willows which have become too big and are in danger of falling and splitting. Each tree is cut down to a 'stool' so that new growth can establish itself lower in the trunk, giving the tree many more years of useful growth.

The reason why there are so many trees lining the banks of a chalkstream like ours is that they provide vital shelter, not only for the angler but also for the river's fly life.

In very open country flies are blown and buffeted around and their journey from and back to the river can be made impossible. The result is that flies hatch, but the females are unable to return to the river to lay their eggs. As a result the water is denied natural re-stocking and a valuable

Through the season banks of silt build up below the Mill Weir; these will be grabbed off at the end of the year

foodstuff for the growing trout is lost. In sheltered conditions, though, the egg-laying females have a much shorter and easier flight back to the water. Those stretches of the River Test below Stockbridge, where deep wooded shelter exists, have never lost their mayfly. Where these woodland barriers protect the stream from northerly winds, the fly life has benefited considerably. The same is true on the Wallop Brook and the Dun, two of the Test's tributaries, which run from west to east in shelter. They have maintained a valuable nucleus of mayfly.

Back in the nineteenth century, when members fished exclusively with the blowline and needed a reasonable breeze to get their flies out on the water, trees along the entire length of the Houghton Club waters were felled to let the breeze in. The introduction of the whipping rod changed all that. My grandfather was able to plant all manner of trees, and place them where they would shelter the water without interfering with the fisherman's back cast.

It was around this time that grandfather created what I believe to be the perfect planting plan for any chalkstream: avenues of trees planted three deep – tall at the back, medium in the middle, with the shorter trees sited some 20 yards from the bank. He was also careful not to allow trees on the western bank to grow too tall; if they were too large they would block out the bright light during the evening rise. We have continued in this vein, planting trees wherever possible. One of our main problems is that not all the land alongside the river belongs to the Club. However, only this year we recovered several more acres and we started replanting trees to provide extra shelter.

You could say that as a result of the Lunns' labours through the years, the Houghton Club waters have been 'bespoke tailored' for the sporting members.

On our waters we have golden, purple and black willow, all of which grow readily from sets. Of the other trees, the alder, the ash, the birch, the poplar and the hawthorn are all indigenous to the Test Valley. One of my favourites is the alder which, if planted correctly near the bank, overhangs the river's edge to produce an attractive lie for trout on a hot summer's day. Such trees go with insects and rising trout and the deep shade helps the angler spot his fish.

Many of the members compliment me on the beauty of our river at the start of the season, some of them remarking on how picturesque the willows are as they wave gently in the summer breeze. Those same members can also be heard cursing every branch and twig when their back cast flips high into a willow and refuses to unsnag itself. Never mind, it's good for the fly tyer in that it enhances his turnover!

The month of March is our last chance to put the finishing touches to the river. This is when we give each of the huts on each Beat a spring-clean. The fishing huts are not used so much nowadays, but in grandfather and father's day the chauffeur, ghillie or keeper would take the fisherman's lunch to the hut and the member would fish upstream to it. Today, access points have improved so most members drive to their Beats and only a thunderstorm drives them into the huts.

This is also the time when the tall nettles, hemlock and long dead spears are burned or cut to avoid the anglers' back casts getting fouled up. There's also the last-minute weed cutting on the side streams and carriers; those weeds will have grown well if the winter has been a mild one. As my father always used to say, 'Cut them now and it will save you endless time in the main weed cut of late April and early May'.

It's also busy on the fish farm at this time as we tend to supply many of the reservoirs and stillwater lakes in March to get them off to an early start. The really commercial fishery boys are open all year round, which to my mind means there's nothing to look forward to after the long winter months.

I personally believe that the close season is a time for repairing, refurbishing and replacing rods, reels and lines, a time for hours at the bench tying flies. As March winds blow it's a time of expectation, a time to muse and dream of long summer days and evenings on the water.

But this is a time missed by the all-year-round stillwater angler who takes fish on New Year's Day with a fancy lure all tied up with Flashabou, tinsels and sparkle yarn.

As March settles in so do the first sights and sounds of spring. First, it's the turn of the redshank whose distinctive 'koral-koral-koral' cry can be heard through the valley. The redshank isn't a true migrant, but it is a bird which nests and stays with us until the late summer, when it flies south for its winter holiday on the coast.

At the end of March there's a race between the sand-martin and the swallow as to which will be the first to arrive in Stockbridge, with the house martin a close third. These are joined by the sandpiper, the chiff-chaff, the warblers and the nightingales, followed in mid-April by the swift and the cuckoo, who all add variety and volume to the dawn chorus.

One unwelcome sight, as far as I'm concerned, is the magpie, a bird which has increased in numbers so rapidly over the years that we could soon hear the last of the dawn chorus. It seems, wherever I travel, the magpies are beginning to outnumber all our other birds. Striking looking though they are, what concerns me is their insatiable appetite for eggs, newly-hatched chicks and even fledglings.

One reason for the alarming increase in the number of magpies is that a high proportion of shoots now rely on the rearing of day-old pheasant chicks and poults rather than wild birds. As a result gamekeepers seem to have relaxed much of their vermin-control, now concentrating more on the fox than other animals and birds – like the magpie – that could endanger young game birds.

As March blows itself out, April, with its uncertain winds and showers, sees the true start of the season.

The winter rainfall has, hopefully, swelled the aquifers, giving us a good, strong flow of water through the summer. Chalkstreams rely almost exclusively on the heavy rains between November and March, which filter through the chalk and greensand to these underground reservoirs. Usually 'Him up there' sees to this, but there are years like 1976 and 1989 when a below-average winter rainfall creates a drought year from midsummer to autumn.

The winter of 1988–9 was one of the driest and mildest on record. By June, the water levels were dropping and the temperatures rising into the

80s with our river-water temperature running at 72°F for days on end. On the Houghton Club waters in 1989 we did little in the way of weed cutting, in an effort to keep the levels up. As the summer progressed we were plagued with yard upon yard of flannel or blanket weed, call it what you like, which seemed to grow visibly every day, suffocating and swamping the ranunculus and other life-supporting river weeds.

Flannel weed is a relatively modern phenomenon which we know is brought on by low water, high temperatures, clear skies and a bright sun. It is a growing, living thing which spreads and multiplies so rapidly it can cover a Beat in a matter of days.

The greatest problem for a riverkeeper is that flannel weed is almost impossible to cut – it's like wire wool – and one of our Beats from Bossington Mill upstream to Lunn's cottage became almost unfishable. The water ran slowly and this curse grew to the surface and lay along it in great streamers. If anyone had hooked a trout on that Beat it would have made straight for this clinging, string-like weed which will break even the strongest nylon, leaving the fly in the trout's mouth.

However, one of the Club's younger members was fishing this Beat and hooked a fish. Rather than be denied it he took to the water when the fish became tangled up in the weed. Holding the 6 lb 8oz brown trout up in triumph, he was heard to remark, 'It's okay, I'm only wet to the waist.'

High water temperatures, like those we experienced in 1989, also affect the fish. They become lethargic and unwilling to rise once the mercury moves into the high 60s; only at dusk do a few fish move freely. I was expecting the grayling to suffer badly, but only a few were seen dying. My father told me that in 1921, which was incredibly hot, he saw many grayling die and he always attributed the decline of the 3 lb grayling to that summer.

No one dislikes good summers, least of all me, but it is essential that our underground water reservoirs are adequately filled by winter rainfall, then there's no problem, whatever kind of summer we get.

The only positive side to hot days and still, warm evenings is that they produce spectacular parades of spinners – the dying males and egg-laying females – night after night, so there's a fair multiplication of the fly life for the next season. In fact, 1989 was a bumper year for fly life, particularly the mayfly.

April is also the time for the first weed cut of the season, a time when I walk the bank of the main river, side streams and carriers and indicate where the odd titivation is necessary to neaten everything on the bank and in the river. The shallow upper river, with its robust growth of ranunculus, celery and starwort, needs more attention than the middle and lower reaches. All these details must be seen to before the waters are stocked and the season's first members arrive, their eyes bright with expectation. I used to say they arrived looking rather maggoty and pale. After a few hours at the water they look ten years younger.

Over the years I have witnessed many radical changes in the Test Valley, not least in the way the waters are stocked and fished.

When I first started keepering the lower water, most of the fisheries in the Test Valley were privately owned, and fished only by the estate owner and his guests. This meant that most waters were fished only during the best times of the season and were, as a consequence, under-fished.

When the Houghton Club was founded, few members fished the waters outside the grannom hatches of April and the mayfly hatches of May and June. Even towards the end of the nineteenth century, some members seldom came down after mayfly, preferring to fish for salmon in Scotland from June onwards. So there was next to no pressure on our waters. Even recently, members have fished for salmon in Iceland and Norway during the summer months, returning to Scotland in August for the Glorious Twelfth and the grouse moors.

Nowadays, most of the fisheries up and down the Test Valley are over-fished, with many stretches, however short, run by syndicates with fee-paying rods who expect their pound of flesh throughout the season. Some of these waters even let out water to half and quarter season rods, packing in as many anglers as possible to make the sport pay. In fact, on several fisheries I supply with Houghton Club trout, every beat has a rod on it throughout the season and every time a poor old trout sticks his nose out of the water, it's bombarded with flies of all shapes and sizes.

I have never credited trout with having much brain, but they are quite quick to learn what is good and not good for them. When there are this many people fishing the waters the trout become very difficult to catch and you simply don't get the best out of them, or the water. Not that I'm suggesting fishing should be made too easy, far from it. On the other hand, there is no virtue in it being totally impossible. Fishing is a hunting game where the expert will always catch more than the novice; a fact best emphasised by the keeper who stocks fairly and infrequently, a formula for angling success any good keeper can quickly work out if he knows his rods and the water.

Too many of today's fishers suffer from what I call 'limititis'; they're not happy unless they catch their limit of four or five fish. And who can blame them? Although fishing is still the poor relation of shooting, they have, after all, paid a lot of money to fish a Beat on the Test and they want value for money.

The easiest way to diagnose limititis in an angler is to ask him about his day on the river. The man who comes into the fishery hut with a beaming smile and full creel usually opens by saying, 'What a lovely day. There was a good hatch of fly, the fish were rising well and that new casting technique of mine made short work of a gusting north-westerly. You know, I didn't once lose a fly in the willows below the weir.'

That same angler on the same Beat on another day, with no fish in his creel, might easily be overheard saying, 'That's the last time I waste my money. There were virtually no fly hatching and I didn't see a fish rise all day. And as for all that bankside vegetation, all I can say is that the keeper should be reprimanded for neglect. If I caught my fly in those weeds and trees once, I must have done it a dozen times.'

At the Houghton Club I can tell at a glance how well the members and their guests have done. That's where the clubroom comes into its own. The member who hasn't seen or caught a fish all day may be despondent and a touch crotchety when he returns there, a tale of woe written all over his face. However, after he has listened to a fellow member who has filled his creel, the despairing angler's expectation rises and he is spurred on to do better the following day.

Sad to say, few of the fisheries on the Test sport a good head of natural wild trout; natural reproduction nowadays will not produce enough fish to meet the needs of anglers. On our water, though, my father introduced the idea of always putting well-grown, three-month-old fry in the water every season to create a good head of native stock. It is a long term plan requiring a programme of fairly heavy stocking to 'top up' the number of wild trout in the river.

However, the higher up the river you go, the more natural regeneration improves. The water above the Houghton Club which is closer to the source of the Test is purer, has a more even temperature and runs through smaller peat deposits, thus reducing the amount of methane in the water.

Although fry stocking is an inexpensive way of getting trout in your river, it can take between three and five years for a wild fish to grow to a reasonable size of around 1 lb 4oz. Not that they have an easy time of it once they're popped in the water. Their greatest enemy is the dabchick, or little grebe, which can decimate a shoal of trout fry.

There are other predators, of course, but although trout certainly eat small fry, I have come across few such cannibals over the years. Pike used to be our greatest problem, but we have now got that completely under control.

It is now April and all is ready for the opening day of the season, which used to coincide with the grannom, the first proper fly of the season. We don't have the massive hatches of grannom that members so enjoyed in grandfather's day, largely because the fly has all but disappeared from the Upper and Middle Test. It does still flourish, however, on the Lower Test and the Avon, but not in the quantities of twenty years ago. I know we lost the grannom because of ill-timed and ill-judged weed cutting; grandfather and father thought the same.

Open season for trout is from 1 April until 31 October and fisheries make their own rules within those dates. At the Houghton Club we choose 14 April until 30 September. Since the massive decline in the grannom few members fish during April, largely because the water is fairly turbid and the hatches of winter and a few spring olives are sparse. The trout, too, have not recovered from overwintering and the meagre food supplies found from October to April. So those members who do come down tend only to walk the water muttering things like, 'I can't wait to get started'. On a rare occasion, though, a member will return with a grin and a small wild brown trout which hasn't yet been through the rigours of spawning.

April is usually a month of grey skies and brisk north-easterly winds, but nature seems able to ignore the kind of weather which keeps us indoors by the fire. These cold conditions always seem to coincide with the flowering of the blackthorn and the first hatches of olives, giving the trout their first sight of the multitudes that share their living quarters.

Early May is a splendid time for the hawthorn fly, a black, long-legged insect that is often blown onto the water, offering the fish their first taste of the larger insects that supplement their diet. I have often been asked why it is that the hawthorn gets blown onto the water, particularly as it is such a robust insect and well able to keep its feet dry. From my observations, it is the combined weight of the copulating male and female that causes them to tumble earthwards in their careless abandon while love-making. Terrestrials, as anglers call them, do not actually hatch from the river, so there is no nymphal stage; the first the fish see of the hawthorn is as a surface fly, which forces them to rise.

Some years, when the wind has not been blowing in the right direction or the breeze has been too light to carry the hawthorn onto the water, I have collected a capful from the bankside comfrey and dropped them, one at a time, onto the water from a bridge above where a member is fishing. Within seconds, first one then another fish rises, to the delight of the rod.

I have known years when these long-legged, shiny beauties have produced as many rising fish during the first fortnight in May as I would normally expect during a good mayfly hatch. Any artificial pattern seems to work, just so long as it's totally black. Unfortunately, the ideal doesn't always happen. In fact, if the weather is cloudy and dull the hawthorn is grounded: they only seem to respond to sunshine and a good westerly blow.

The coming of the Mayfly is more than an incident in the fisherman's year. It is an event of nature.
John Waller Hills, *A Summer on the Test*, 1924

As is the tradition with the Houghton Club, the members tend to come down in force for mayfly. The first of these flies begin to show around 14 May, between 4pm and 6pm. It is only a small hatch to begin with, increasing daily and reaching its peak towards the end of May, with the spent gnat returning to the water on every fine, still afternoon and evening.

So much, though, depends on the mild or harsh weather of the winter months. It can affect the timing of the hatch tremendously. Years ago, the mayfly seemed to be much more of a June fly. I believe that the succession of mild winters over the last five years or so has meant that the nymphs have matured faster and hatched those few days earlier. In 1989 the mild winter and fine, sunny weather saw every mayfly that hatched returning to the water; one of those rare sights that makes you stare in absolute wonder.

Since as far back as I can remember, this time has been known as 'duffers' fortnight', and rightly so. If the angler cannot catch a fish then, he will never catch one. On the river-bank, it gives me a lot of joy to see an elderly gent's face light-up as I tie what looks like a yellow canary onto the end of his cast.

This is a wonderful time for me; a time when the lifecycle of the river and its fly life comes together in one glorious explosion. There's the emerging nymph, the fly on the water, the dance of the males, the courtship, the egg-laying, the ovipositing females and the dying spent gnats, fluttering their last on the water as fish after fish rises to gorge itself on these large, tasty morsels.

Some fishers grumble about the mayfly from time to time. 'It's too easy,' they say, 'we would be better off without it. I much prefer fishing with the small fly.' It can be frustrating too: after all, why should a fish take your fly from among the hundreds of naturals on the water? The strange thing is that it often does.

Without the mayfly, May can be a quiet month, especially if the days are warm and sunny during the second half of the month. The hawthorn is over and hatches of iron blues and olives may be plentiful but the flies are on the water for such a short time, the trout seldom get a chance to rise. In contrast, the mayfly will hatch whatever the weather; the time has come and they must emerge, whether they be greeted by rain or shine.

On rainy, dull days mayfly tend to spend more time on the water, struggling out of their shucks and fluttering their wings to dry them so that they can become airborne and reach the safety of the nearby trees. Many's the year I have stood above one of the weirs on the Houghton Club water on such a day and watched helplessly as countless mayfly have gone through the sluices and drowned, never to reproduce.

They also provide the bird life with quite a feast, whether the flies are on the water or fluttering for the sanctuary of a nearby tree. Suddenly, it seems, our 15 miles of the Test Valley becomes a hive of activity. Ducks and the first of their young scoot over the water like speed skaters, chasing each fly as it struggles to take to the air. At this point of emergence, sparrows and chaffinches swoop down and pick them off the water, closely followed by the starlings who hunt around the trees for the adult flies. But perhaps the most spectacular sight of all – one that sums up this glorious moment in the life of my river – is the build-up to the fall of mayfly spinners.

On a fine, warm afternoon the dancing males gather by every tree and hedgerow to perform Nature's Ballet. It's a time for love-making as the females leave the shelter of the trees to give themselves to some fortunate mayfly Nureyev. The combined weight of the male and female takes them to the ground and seconds later the air is thick with fertilised females as they start their migration up river to lay their eggs.

In good years, when the mayfly hatch is prolific, every fly-eating fish has a chance to recover some of the condition it lost after spawning, the rigours of winter and meagre rations.

Many of my members feel that after mayfly the fish are gorged and disinclined to rise for some time. This is not entirely true. After all, we like to have three meals a day, so does a trout. To me it's just a question of the fish getting their eye in again. It is also worth noting that so many fish are taken during mayfly, there are fewer trout in the water, and many of those that are there are the 'ones that got away' during duffers' fortnight.

Mind you, from the trout's point of view the days immediately after mayfly must be quite bewildering. One day the river is groaning with the weight of these large, succulent insects; the very next day the surface is empty of all but minuscule flies which individually don't offer a snack, never mind a three-course meal.

After mayfly the river takes on a more peaceful look. There are a few olives hatching for an hour or so after midday and in the evening, if the weather is set fair, the pale watery dun will be the one fly to hatch that offers us some fishing, with spinners of each fly tempting a few fish to rise.

But this slack period doesn't last long. With mayfly off the menu, other hatches of daytime flies are also dwindling, numerous trout have been caught and removed by anglers and, yes, things are much quieter. But I promise you, a caperer by day and a sedge and ginger quill in the evening, fished with as much patience as you can muster, will take good fish.

For most people June is the start of summer proper, a time for long evenings outdoors stretched idly in a hammock.

For riverkeepers, June is one of the busiest summer months, because it heralds the major weed cut of the season. By now the river is a forest of ranunculus, water celery and mare's-tail as well as deeper-rooted potamogetons or pond weeds. The bulrush, too, is thrusting upwards. Cutting it is hard, physical and highly skilled work, but it is vital if the river is to fish well for the rest of the season.

Without weed a river such as ours is a desolate place, and as much as we keepers curse the main weed cut of the season, the plant life of any river needs nurturing, for without it the fishing would be a disaster.

Weed performs many functions in a river. First, it controls the height of the water and its direction of flow and is invaluable in low water years like 1989. It also provides a great sanctuary for river life, particularly for fish. Without the various forms of plant life in a river, there would be no insects. No insects means no food and no food would mean the trout would die of starvation.

Many of the tools used in grandfather and father's day are still around, in particular the hand scythe, the long pole scythe and the chain scythe. One modern addition to the keeper's armoury is the motorised weed cutting boat, which is a good tool for clearing out heavily weeded stretches of water but is not, to my mind, selective enough.

By the third week of June the major weed cut of the season is over. Apart from it being hard and hot work, the weed cut is a time when we are besieged by what I call the great irritants of a riverkeeper's life. Fortunately, on the Test, we are not plagued by the helicopter-sized mosquitoes of some of the better Scottish salmon waters. However, we do have the horsefly, which is very definitely the plague of this riverkeeper's life. It always seems to be around when I'm up to my waist in the river, shirtsleeves rolled above the elbow, moving a heavy scythe through a bed of ranunculus in midstream. It's then that a horsefly lands on my arm so softly that I don't feel it until it stings me. By then it's too late to brush it off and, almost as I watch, the arms swells and I know I'm in for a painful night.

After the main June weed cut we re-stock the river so that there are a few 'new faces' around. This mid-season stocking sees more rainbows than brown trout being introduced. Experience has shown that rainbow trout are better value from July onwards than they are in the early part of the season, mostly because in the second half of the year they seem to rise more freely than the brown trout.

The idea of having fish that were all female seemed good, mostly because it avoided the tremendous losses of male trout during the winter months. During the breeding season – which runs from November to December – male trout fight freely, literally tearing one another to pieces in their randy state. However, after 15 years of experimentation and the use of oestrogen, the female hormone, I am still undecided whether it is an advantage or a disadvantage to breed and stock with entirely female rainbows. For quite a few females do die becoming, for want of a more scientific phrase, egg-bound and unable to get rid of their ova. So it seems like sod's law whatever you choose to do. Overall, though, you realise that not every yearling you produce will turn into a catchable trout. Fish of any age have a nasty habit of dying on you, albeit from their make-up as much as from disease.

On the early mornings on the Test in September the mist converts the scene into a fairyland of beauty. The willows are yellowing and all is seen through a steamy veil which clears up as the sun gets higher.
E. A. Barton, *An Album of the Chalk Streams*, 1946

JULY and August are fairly relaxed months for a riverkeeper; they're the months when our main task is to tidy up the river and its banks. This means our fishers can enjoy long days and evenings without the aggravation of overgrown bankside vegetation grabbing at their flies. We also make sure the river is shorn of the floating islands of weed that create difficult currents and prevent the angler floating a drag-free dry fly down to an expectant fish. Keeping the river open and fishable is the order of the day.

One necessary job in July is the manicuring of our banks, a task which in the past twenty years has been eased considerably by the invention of more mechanised techniques. In grandfather's day, bankside vegetation was cut with a mowing scythe; nowadays we use a mini-tractor and flail.

Of all the bankside tasks, 'topping', as we call it, is probably the most important. In simple terms, it is all about pruning the faster growing bankside vegetation. Spears need topping, as do some of the flowering plants like agrimony and willow-herb, which can grow anything up to 6ft tall during the sunshine and showers of May and June.

We tend not to touch sedge, because as it grows it tends to fold itself over; it seems to be one of nature's more tidy plants. Top it and you're asking for trouble, because if you prune it, it will grow back all spiky, doubling in size and causing all sorts of problems for the anglers.

In grandfather and father's day the keepers used reap hooks and long-handled slashers to top the banks. Now we use the same kind of hedge trimmers that can be found in any gardener's armoury.

We also have a mini weed cut in July, which is a time when we are able to assess the sort of water we think we are going to be dealing with by the end of the season. In a low water year like 1989, it is essential to leave as much weed in the river as possible to keep the level up. If you cut everything in July, particularly in the shallows, the water-level will drop to a trickle and the river will very quickly become unfishable.

Weed cutting on our part of the river is mostly done with a chain scythe – which is a string of knives stretched across the water and pulled by two keepers at either end of a rope. It's a good way of trimming the crop and it helps to get over the ground more quickly. We also use a pole scythe, a razor-sharp sickle mounted on an 18ft pole which is wielded either from a boat or the bank. It's an accurate tool which enables us to cut channels and blocks of weed at different points on each beat. By doing this we are able to 'tailor' the water to suit both the trout and our fishers.

On my river what I tend to do is leave channels in the shallows and blocks of weed in the main water course. On a wide band of shallows I create two lines of weed and three runs: one under each bank and one in the middle of the river. We always ensure that enough weed is left so that it can grow up and out of the water, thus providing ladders for the egg-laying flies to crawl down. This pattern of weed cutting also offers sanctuary for the fish.

On the Houghton Club waters we have the sort of shallows which are not frightfully long, with deep water in front, then shallows, then deep water again. On such shallows I like to leave a block of weed right across the river, which means that fish in the deeper water have a constant flow of nymphs washed out from the weed.

Nature, too, plays its part in July, what with the growth of ranunculus, celery, carrot weed, starwort and the early flush of mare's-tail. This is also the time when the pond weeds are growing, providing their marvellous filtering qualities and bringing a new, crystal clarity to the river.

What with topping and the mini weed cut, all of us are on the water every day, so July is a time when as keepers we are looking at which fish are where on the river. This is all the more important at this time because the days and evenings are longer, fish are rising all over our river, and there are as many members and guests down as there are during mayfly.

As the water has cleared around this time, we are also on the lookout for the odd pike in the river. We remember where we have seen them and store this information away until the winter months when we patrol the water with the electric fisher and take out unwanted predators.

For members of the Houghton Club, July heralds the time when a trout will often take a nymph in preference to a dry fly. It is when the trout in our shallows can be seen 'tailing', or rooting about in the stones for shrimp and nymphs, or grabbing at the caddis larvae which are crawling awkwardly from the sanctuary of one stone to another. Such fish are difficult to catch, mostly because they seldom look up to the surface and you have to wait for the trout to become inactive before accurately dropping a Caperer over its nose.

I remember many years ago, stalking Sheepbridge Shallows with Sir Laurence Dunne one still, warm July morning. There were lots of small wild trout tailing as we waded slowly up to them with the trees and sun at our backs for maximum cover. I was searching the water for a catchable fish over the Houghton Club's 1 lb 4oz limit.

Done well, stalking is a very slow, painstaking business, because all too often you can scare smaller fish, which in turn will zip through the water and disturb the fish above them.

On this day, though, I spotted one wild trout of around 2 lb casually drifting back to intercept one nymph, then another, as these emerging insects were washed out of the weed cover upstream of the fish.

Tying on a Caperer and remembering that the fish needs to see the fly fall to attract him up from his underwater larder, Sir Laurence flicked his fly expertly to within an inch of the trout's nose. After three or four chucks it was obvious that the trout wasn't going to bother with the effort of rising to a surface fly, so we switched to our old friend, the Orange and Partridge Nymph.

This fly, among others, was one of my grandfather's creations, one that we as a family have favoured over many other nymph patterns. Tied in sizes from a 16 to longshank 8 it has accounted for the catching of innumerable trout on the Houghton Club waters. The larger tying was father's idea for catching large trout that were taking minnows in the shallows.

I called out 'You' as the trout took Sir Laurence's fly – this is the word used by keepers past and present to indicate to their rod that he should strike, particularly when the fly isn't easy to see. The shout doesn't need to be over-loud or violent, otherwise it produces a strike like a horse kicking, and you can say goodbye to the fly. Although lost flies were a frequent occurrence in the days of gut casts, it's rare today since the adoption of nylon.

Quite often, keepers find themselves fishing with rods who are far from expert or, worse still, incapable of seeing a rise even on the surface. Such anglers need a loudish 'You' to get them to strike. It's neat and quick and catches a lot of fish.

All members of the Houghton Club are used to the call and respond immediately, especially when fishing an upstream nymph. Some anglers don't like the 'You', so you avoid a reprimand for being presumptuous if you can manage to stifle it. Others ask you to call; it's all about knowing your fisherman and fitting in with his likes and dislikes.

I have always maintained that any fool can throw a nymph upstream to a fish, but it takes a good man like Sir Laurence Dunne to tell when the fish has taken it.

So how do you tell? It is easy if you can see your fish and watch his every move, because most times you can see the fish move across, open its mouth and take the nymph as it turns. The secret here is never to cast the nymph directly over the fish, but always to cast to one side of it so that you can see the take as it moves to intercept the fly.

Nymph fishing also requires a certain amount of patient experimentation. Sometimes the trout will take a nymph cast on its nose in much the same way as it would a dry fly. Other times, you may need to cast further upstream of the fish to give the weighted nymph a chance to sink to the depth at which the fish is feeding. It's really all a matter of observation.

When it comes to fishing the trout which is not visible, the angler must use his nymph differently and with more skill. If you don't see the trout 'bulge' to the fly, breaking the surface as it rises, then you have to rely almost entirely on seeing the cast being drawn down through the surface film.

The best way of helping you see this 'draw' is to grease the cast – probably at 15-minute intervals – from the end of the fly line to within 6in. of the nymph, or whatever depth you want to fish it. As a result, the ungreased section of cast will sink with the nymph and leave the greased section visible and floating on the surface. Immediately you see any movement on this greased section of your cast, strike. Sure, your nymph may have snagged a piece of weed, but any movement of the visible cast should prompt a reaction from the flyfisher; you should never, ever, miss the slightest movement. It could make the difference between being fishless and having a full creel.

August brings us to our final weed cut of the season; a time when we make sure that every beat has a good amount of fishable water.

At this time of year we are beginning to lose fishermen to the grouse moors and salmon lochs of Scotland, so it's a time when I like to take my annual busman's holiday, which is a couple of weeks' salmon fishing on the River Spey. Those two weeks take away the staleness, so when I return to Stockbridge I am totally rejuvenated and looking forward to seeing the season through.

In August and September there are still a few people wanting fish, particularly the stillwater fisheries who stay open longer than we do.

And so we come to September, which for me is one of the best times of the year outside of mayfly, although it can be a law unto itself. Flows are dropping away, the water is crystal clear and some of the trout have passed their A level in survival, making them particularly difficult to catch. So when I'm out with a member I keep him at it, casting steadily and changing flies often for hours on end. September days are challenging, so persistence can often catch a fish. It is also the month when a nymph is more likely to take a fish than a dry fly. My feeling is that even the better educated trout will fall for this ploy.

At this time of year the fish are easily spooked and a heavily delivered cast, or even the movement of the rod, will instantly put them down. So it pays to try something different: kneel rather than stand when casting and fish with a finer point on the tippet. The fly hatches are quite good, with olives and iron blues by day, pale wateries and blue winged olives by night. The days are also shorter so daytime and evening fishing run into one another.

At the Houghton Club we take a Beat for daytime fishing, break for tea at 5pm, change Beats for the evening and eat supper at the end of the day. To my mind, fishing and meals always present a problem.

September can be a magical time, particularly if the full moon comes on or near 7 September. Known as the harvest moon, it coincides with the emergence of the pupa of the needle brown sedge, which skitters across the surface to reach the safety of the bank. If the evening is fine and still and the moonlight at the right angle on the water, you are guaranteed some of the greatest dry fly fishing of your life.

I remember one night on the Grosvenor Water with Sir Laurence Dunne when conditions were near-perfect. As is always the case when fishing under the harvest moon our eyes were strained watching for the tiny wake created by the needle brown pupae and our ears were listening for the audible kissing or sucking sound of the trout as they rose to intercept the insects.

At the first sight and sound of a rise, Sir Laurence positioned himself upstream of the fish, ready to throw his line downstream and to the left of the rise and over-cast a foot or so beyond the fish. In the meantime I parted the rushes close to where the trout was feeding so that I could guide Sir Laurence's cast and retrieve. In the dim light shed by the moon fish are less shy, which means you can literally get close enough to reach out and touch them.

Sir Laurence cast his fly accurately and lightly onto the water and waited for my commentary. 'Lift your rod now, Sir Laurence, slowly now, keep lifting, the fly's over its tail now, keep lifting. . . . You.' At the 'You' command he lifted into a fine brown trout of 2 lb 6oz.

That night – and I mean night because fishing the harvest moon seldom starts before 10pm and can go on into the following morning – even Sir Laurence managed to miss one or two fish. Not through any fault of his, I hasten to add. Fishing downstream in this manner means that the strike drags the fly away from the fish, as opposed to upstream fishing where the fly is jagged back into the trout's face.

All is not lost if a fish is missed, either, because for some reason the same fish will come again and again, so obsessed are they with these emerging pupae.

That night Sir Laurence hooked and grassed his last fish, a fine 3 lb 2oz brown trout, just as the Stockbridge Town Hall clock struck twelve. 'What do you think, Mick, should we enter this one in the book for today or tomorrow?'

By 30 September, I have to admit, I'm wondering where the time has gone. It barely seems a moment ago that I was getting excited over the mayfly. Remarks such as, 'This is my last day, Mick,' and 'See you next year, Mick, God willing. Hope you winter well,' bring it all to a close.

In October fly life abounds, which I believe is nature's way of making sure that the fish reach the peak of condition in preparation for the long winter months ahead. It is the month when I offer the grayling fishing on our waters to the local angling clubs and the Grayling Society. It gives them the opportunity to fish what I believe to be the best part of the River Test, and with the bonus of the odd rainbow thrown in – there is no close season for this American immigrant – it's probably the highlight of their year.

And here we are again at the end of yet another season. The rods are packed away and swapped for the gun. The clubroom at the Grosvenor Hotel is cleared and the handsome John Wootton clock on the mantelshelf allowed to wind down. For us riverkeepers another year is just beginning. It is our job to prepare the water and the trout for the coming April so that the Houghton Club's members and their guests will enjoy the kind of fishing that will occupy their conversations throughout the season.

Me selecting fish for restocking from Black Lake stewpond

Playing and netting a fish below the weed rack at the top of Machine Beat

V

THEN AND NOW

————————◆◆◆————————

I HAVE lived in this valley for more than sixty years and sometimes it's hard to believe that we ever pumped our water from a well, listened to the Grand National on a crystal set or 'cat's whisker' wireless as it was known, walked the three miles to Stockbridge down an unmade road, and only had oil lamps and candles for lighting.

Fishermen and fishing have changed, too. When grandfather arrived at the Houghton Club in 1886 and took over as Head Keeper in January 1887, flyfishers could be roughly divided into two categories: the blowers, who used the blowline and a natural fly; and the whippers, who used the whipping rod and the artificial wet fly. In 1887 the members of the Houghton Club were still blowers, although many anglers had turned to the whipping rod and the artificial dry fly for their pursuit of the trout in our chalkstreams.

To the modern eye, the illustrations of those late nineteenth century members of the Houghton Club must look extraordinary compared with today's flyfishers. But then the members were gentlemen of leisure whose lives were carefully ordered to take advantage of the sporting year, from January and the foxhunt through the grannom in April and the mayfly in June to the grouse moors or salmon rivers in August. When they came down to Stockbridge their elegance when they set off for the river must have astounded the locals. Picture the scene: thirteen top-hatted and frock-coated gentlemen accompanied by their servants, or ghillies chosen from among the local men. When they arrived at their chosen Beat on the river their ghillies would put up their blowlines, which were from 18 to 20ft long bamboo cane. Each of these had a reel filled with an undressed silk line fitted to the butt of the rod, a gut cast and hook attached to the end of the line.

Once the blowline was ready the ghillies netted a box of grannom, mayflies or caperers (which are summer sedges), depending on the time of year, and impaled the mature insect on the hook: two grannom flies were recommended, but only one mayfly or caperer. The member would then work out 30–40 yards of line in the wind, making sure not to let the line or the fly touch the water until the fly was blown over a rising fish, at which moment it was guided expertly onto the water.

At the time, many members considered it was 'bad form' to let the line touch the water, even when the fly was put before a fish, because it was believed that undressed silk rotted if it got wet. But there was one major disadvantage to this practice: on wild, blustery May days it was impossible to control the 30 yards of line blowing in the wind and accurately lay the fly on the water. My grandfather, however, changed the members' tactics when he discovered that if he laid a few yards of line on the water it steadied the fly and, as a result, deceived and killed more fish. Blowline fishing, as I have discovered, is not as simple as it sounds, mainly because the up and down draughts at the water's surface tend to make the fly skitter about uncontrollably.

Today, the Houghton Club is the revered home of dry fly fishing. However, up until 1887 members used almost any method to catch trout, including spinning with live minnows in the weirs. This meant that when members were down, the keepers were obliged to place cans of live minnows at the weirs.

According to most authorities, spinning and worming were banned from the Houghton Club waters by 1890. It is also believed that Arthur Gilbey at last persuaded the members to adopt the whipping rod – the greenheart forerunner of today's lightweight fly rods – and the artificial fly in, or around, 1893. Some members, however, had already experimented and mastered these new-fangled devices, as is shown by Richard Penn's notes and hints entered in the clubroom book in 1829:

> In whipping with the artificial fly remember that when you have drawn your fly out of the water it must have time to make the whole circuit, and be at one time straight behind you before it can be driven out straight before you. If you give it the forward impulse too soon you will hear a crack. Take this as a hint that your fly is probably gone to griefs.
>
> Never throw with a long line when a short one will answer your purpose. The most difficult fish to hook is one which is rising at three-fourths of the distance to which you can throw. Even when at

the extent of your distance you have a better chance because in this case when you do reach him your line will be straight and the intermediate failures will not alarm him when you do not.

I sometimes wonder how Richard Penn would have coped with the changes that have taken place in the Club's rod room at the Grosvenor Hotel. How would he have dealt with the move away from the early split cane rods, which took the place of whipping rods, towards the first metal fly rods, then glass-fibre and now carbon and boron rods? All this as well as the amazingly wide selection of lengths and actions they offer combined with their phenomenal light weight.

Other vital aspects of the flyfishers armoury have changed dramatically over the past one hundred years. It's a long time since I have had to dress a silk fly line to make it float, because most members of the Houghton Club have switched to high tech fly lines with built-in buoyancy bubbles and more serviceable plastic coverings. I have to admit that I have never mourned the passing of the gut cast – which needed to be kept carefully in a damp cloth to retain its flexibility – and welcome the finer, stronger nylon casts of today.

When the whipping rod was first adopted by members the majority fished a team of submerged wet flies rather than a single dry fly.

Here on the Test in the early 1800s at Longparish, which is about 6 miles upstream of our water, Colonel Hawker and the Reverend Durnford were expert wet fly anglers with the whipping rod. As I recall it, Hawker used only two flies – a Yellow Dun on the end or 'point' of his cast and a small Red Palmer on the dropper, which was tied on to his cast about 2ft above his point fly – and in so doing killed an enormous number of fish. Durnford, however, chose from a selection of about a dozen wet flies, which were mostly nondescript-looking things with a simple body and hackle. Hawker and Durnford's artificial flies were, no doubt, created to mimic the shape and movement of the nymphs and drowned mature insects of the Test: and I am sure they would work as well today as they did then.

In simple terms the difference between the wet and dry fly fishermen is that the former 'fishes the stream', searching every pocket, riffle and glide with a team of sunken flies cast either downstream or down and across the stream. The dry fly fisherman 'fishes the rise', by casting a single dry fly upstream to a particular fish he can see rising.

The change over to fishing upstream with a single dry fly to a specific, rising trout was largely brought about in the late 1800s and early 1900s by the writings of Frederic Halford. He insisted that for any flyfisher to succeed, he had to have a box of tiny artificials, each tied to closely imitate the natural flies the trout were feeding on. Halford and his many avid followers were purists and they laid down the basic rules of dry fly fishing, which have survived on our chalkstreams to this day. The only addition – which at the time created a bitter debate and divided the flyfishing world – was the development of the artificial nymph by G. E. M. Skues. He rightly reasoned that a major part of the trout's diet had to be made up of the nymphs of the various aquatic insects found in our chalkstreams. There are still people today who will never use a nymph, believing it to be unsporting. I have to disagree with them.

My earliest recollection of the debate about how to catch fish with the dry fly goes back to the mid-1930s. At that time the talk was about accuracy of presentation with an imitation that most closely resembled the natural insect. To a man, these anglers followed Halford's simple rules: always cast upstream to a fish and only with a single dry fly; never cast to a trout unless it is rising to the natural fly; never encroach on another's water. Simple though these rules are, my feeling is that whether you use a wet fly, dry fly or a nymph, you should never use a method likely to spoil the sport of other anglers.

Halford died in 1914, and what a great man he was, a 'legend'. His studies of the live insects and his creation of so many artificial fly patterns are represented in his eloquent writings. Even today these stand as great works; I don't think we will ever see the equal of his *Dry-Fly Fishing in Theory and Practice, Dry Fly Entomology* and his *Modern Development of the Dry Fly*, published four years before his death.

My grandfather started tying flies in 1916 at the age of 54, under the tuition of Mr E. J. Power, a Houghton Club member and expert fly tier. In those days, most fly tiers created their artificials the Halford way, making them as accurate to the naturals as was humanly possible with twists of fur and feather. Within a year or two, however, grandfather noticed that beautiful though these creations were, to his mind they did not look as accurate from the trout's underwater point of view as they should.

Halford dressed his flies so that they looked as lifelike as possible on the water, evolving in 1910 a set of artificials that were exact to the last detail, right down to differentiating the sexes of the natural. According to grandfather, though, Halford's artificials ignored the trout and how it viewed the fly, so he set about proving the point by creating artificials which looked realistic to the trout's eyes.

To ensure absolute accuracy, he would spend countless hours staring into his aquarium. Here he could observe the way the feet of the mature winged insect dimpled the surface of the water when it emerged and rested, waiting for its wings to become operational. He continued his observations down on the riverside, watching spinners as they either went down in the water to lay their eggs or, like the mayfly, pierced the surface and injected their eggs into the water, shaking and trembling with the effort of ovipositing.

His observations and long hours at the vice created forty patterns, including flies which feature in every dry flyfisher's box today such as the Caperer, Houghton Ruby, Lunn's Particular, Yellow Boy, Sherry Spinner and Hackle Bluewing. As Sir Laurence Dunne once said after trying one of grandfather's new creations, 'I don't know how the old wizard worked that out but he did and it works like a dream'.

He took these notes and observations back with him to his fly tying bench and translated them into a range of quite revolutionary artificial duns, spinners and nymphs, covering the many insects indigenous to the Middle Test. He discovered, among other things, that a hackled artificial fly worked better than Halford's winged patterns, which were accurate right down to the exact wing form and size, but did little to impress the trout. Instead, grandfather created loosely dressed flies, described by John Waller Hills in his book *River Keeper* as 'indefinite and shapeless, without form or modelling, legs and wings mingled in a confused whirl of feathers': these fooled even the most experienced trout.

Since grandfather and father's day there has been a lot of 'jaw' talked about what fly to use and when and the magazines are full of articles about this natural and that, this artificial representation and that. I, however, have devised a much simpler set of rules, designed to take the mystique out of flyfishing, without taking away any of the enjoyment.

These basic, and by no means rigid rules about which fly to use, where and how, are borne out by the way members of the Houghton Club consistently take good fish from their waters. They have proved conclusively over the years that the old and hallowed concept that only an exact copy of the natural will catch a fish is complete rubbish. To those people who argue to the contrary, I show the book in the clubroom, where on a single day every member has taken six fish, and all on different fly patterns.

As far as I'm concerned, it's the size of fly that matters when it comes to that moment when, with furrowed brow, the angler looks into his box and ponders over which fly to tie on the end of his cast. He checks the water, straining his eyes to distinguish the natural on the water that is so avidly being sipped down by the trout. 'So what is that fly?' he asks himself, and 'Do I have an accurate imitation?'

There are a few exceptions to the rule that size is pretty well everything:

no matter what you use during a fall of black gnat or hawthorn flies, the trout will be interested only in very small or large black flies. The trout are also highly selective when there is a fall of sherry spinners – the artificial seems to work better than any other small fly – and if you toss a small artificial at a trout who is rising to the mayfly it will be ignored.

Outside of those exceptions the following rules on size of fly rather than pattern seem to work every time. For example, if you see a fish rising consistently, chuck him a small fly. If there's a fish rising to fly you can see hatching on the water, cast it a small, but hackled dry fly. When you see spinners preparing to fall and spot a fish making sipping rises, then use a spinner pattern. Finally, if you come across a fish who rises only occasionally – a 'oncer' – a big fly like a Caperer, Brown Sedge or Wulff will work.

I haven't delved into the entomology of fly fishing because although a knowledge of the natural flies which hatch through the season adds a new and fascinating dimension to flyfishing, it is not absolutely necessary. It is, nevertheless, an absorbing facet of our sport.

The other aspect of dry fly fishing where I disagree with Halford and the purists is in the idea that you should only cast to a visible rising fish. Although I can think of nothing better than fishing for a rising trout, there are plenty of days when you never see a free-rising fish. On such days, particularly from June (after mayfly) to August, when rising fish are hard to find during the daylight hours, a pair of Polaroid spectacles cuts out the surface glare and enables you to search the water for a likely fish feeding below the surface on nymphs. Providing you see it before it sees you, there's every chance you will tempt it with a floating fly or a nymph below the surface. I sometimes wonder if Halford's or my grandfather's flies would have been created differently if Polaroids had been around in their day.

I can remember many July days when I have accompanied an angler during the daytime session and not seen one fish rise. I have, however, spotted several in the water, moving to right and left, as they intercept the nymphs tumbling down to them on the current. Rather than drop a nymph on its nose I have persuaded the angler to try each fish with a large dry fly, only for the fish to rise – perhaps for the first time that day – and confidently grasp the fly in its mouth. It is tremendous sport, and for me there is nothing unsporting or unethical about it. Unfortunately, not all the anglers I fish with are good at what I call 'looking in' the water; young eyes definitely have the advantage here.

Over the past thirty years my simple dry fly rules have worked almost every time. Looking through the book in the clubroom, it is a matter of fact that more fish have been taken on the Red or the Grey Wulff than any other pattern, followed in popularity by the Caperer and the Little Brown Sedge. The Wulff was first introduced to members by Lewis Douglas, the US Ambassador, who arrived in the clubroom one morning, propped his box of Wulffs on the mantelpiece and invited members to try the pattern. It was an instant hit, both with the members and the trout, and I remember my father was inundated with orders from members to tie the pattern on small hooks.

In recent years, fewer fish have been taken on the Houghton Club waters with the kind of tiny artificials recommended by Frederic Halford. Some anglers believe that the success of the larger fly, like the Wulff, has something to do with today's stocked fish being less selective. This can't actually be true because our wild fish fall for the Wulff just as readily as the stock fish. Certainly the tackle we use today is more sophisticated, particularly when you compare today's almost invisible, ultra-fine, double-strength nylon casts with the gut casts of thirty years ago. No, I think that it's the size of fly first, pattern second; after all, my friend Oliver Kite caught hundreds of fish on what he called 'a nymph', which was little more than a bare hook. I even overheard one fisherman – not on our waters, I hasten to add – swear by what he called his Pellet Fly, whatever that was.

My advice to anglers is always to have patience and offer the trout a selection of flies before giving up on it. If it's a really difficult fish and refuses every fly in your box, spit on the fly and see if the trout is prepared to take the fly just under the surface; nine times out of ten it will. Purists may not approve of this method, but it can make the difference between a blank day and fish in the bag.

I think the 'upstream only' dictum laid down by Halford is more a matter of commonsense than etiquette. I must say, though, that I disapprove thoroughly of the 'chuck it and chance it' flyfisher who fishes the water with a dry fly, starts off with an upstream cast on the surface and allows the fly to drift downstream before retrieving it as a submerged fly. That, to me, is very definitely unsporting.

Downstream dry fly fishing is in my view allowable when the current and the position of the angler preclude an effective, drag-free upstream cast. In this circumstance, I think it is okay for the angler to stand upstream of the rising fish and cast his line downstream with enough of a belly in the line to allow it to float down to the trout without the current causing drag. The 'downstream drifter', as I call him, is the angler who will pretty well always take fish where there is a mixed current of fast and slow water caused by an encroaching bank of weed or the current-dividing stanchion of a bridge.

Another case where it would be permissible to fish dry fly downstream is when fishing a Sedge pattern – particularly during the harvest moon. This is when the trout is likely to take a fly that is drawn across the surface, imitating the way that the pupae of the needle brown make a dash for the security of the bank.

Halford was right, though, when he explained that an accurate cast catches more trout than an inaccurate one. As G. S. Marryat replied when asked by Francis Francis what fly he was using with such success, 'It's not the fly, it's the driver'.

Over the past one hundred years or so, three generations of Lunn have coached, bullied and taught members and guests about the importance of letting the fly land so that the fish sees it. It is not only very satisfying to cast a fly accurately on the nose of a rising fish and have it come confidently to the fly, but also vital when the water is literally plastered with naturals.

Mind you, I sometimes feel that this preoccupation with casting accuracy is a little strong. I have witnessed a good many inaccurate anglers catch quite a number of fish and it has often been my lot to accompany such anglers, ensuring that their visit to the river is as pleasurable as possible.

These are the flyfishers whose nylon casts grow wind knots within minutes of arriving at the water, whose back casts always manage to grab hold of a shrub or thistle, whose heavy delivery always prompts me to remark, 'He should have seen that one, Sir'. But somehow the trout can be kind to the beginner. I have to admit that when fishing with a novice I find myself talking to the fish under my breath, willing it to take the fly, and as if by a miracle, it sometimes does.

Mind you, the novice is a great walker, rather than stalker of trout. I can't count the times I have suggested that a rod cast his fly from a particular spot on the bank, remarking that he must not get too close because of the light. 'Make your cast a little bit longer,' I explain, only to have to retrieve the angler's fly from a thistle, a few yards behind him. 'Take one step nearer, then,' I suggest helpfully.

I then find I have made a fatal mistake as with each cast, the angler takes another step forward. This culminates in him asking, 'Where is the fish now, Mick?'

'Just under your rod tip, Sir.'

Looking back over the past 30 years, and most certainly before that, I do believe that fishermen made dry fly fishing too difficult and gave the impression that it was a far superior way of fishing in every way to any other. But those flyfishing aesthetes have almost disappeared over the years, particularly since the advent of syndicated fisheries where every rod expects, even demands, that they catch their bag limit on every visit. Etiquette seems to go by the board in achieving that objective; to my mind there is no shame in leaving the river having been defeated; the next day is sure to be a better one.

Small, day ticket, put and take stillwater trout fisheries have only come into existence within the last thirty years. Many of them advertise that they stock larger than average trout and they live off their reputations for this. I'm not a great fan of these man-made stillwater fisheries, but if they introduce more people to the fine art of flyfishing, there's no harm in them. However, some of their so-called flies, like the Dog Nobbler, leave me speechless.

Although I do not stock the Houghton Club waters with many monster fish – from experience they fight less hard than smaller trout – the average size of fish we stock has increased over the years.

When the Club was formed in 1822, the minimum weight limit for fish was 1 lb and many years passed before that was raised, first to 1 lb 4oz, then to 1 lb 8oz. Up to the late 1800s stocking took place less frequently, with members relying more on the native trout in the river: they also caught fewer fish. A more liberal stocking of the water with farm-reared trout was something my father introduced in the 1930s as a way of supplementing the number of wild native fish with larger trout. Unfortunately, the Second World War brought about a shortage of horseflesh, with which to feed the trout in the stewponds – it was in greater demand to feed people in the cities – and as a consequence the minimum weight limit was reduced to 1 lb 4oz; it has stayed at that ever since. The positive side of the minumum weight rule is that members always have the chance of taking a better class of wild fish. These are the result of our continuous stocking over the years with three-month-old trout fry, which do well in the Middle and Upper Test.

Since my father's time as Head Keeper, the average size of the trout caught on the Houghton Club waters has remained fairly constant, at just above 2 lb. However, in the year he retired as Head Keeper, my father had a record year, with an average weight of 2 lb 8oz and more fish caught than in any previous season. I never asked him, but I felt he wanted to go out on a really high note . . . and why not?

My father was a great believer, as I am, in being selective over the brood stock in the fish farm, working on the principle that like breeds like. The trout we breed in the fish farm have, over the years, improved in condition and size as a direct result of the invention and quality of pelleted trout food. During the development of these foods we had a number of problems, as well as a few dead fish, but the pellet food we now use comes very close to providing the trout with a complete diet.

As my father always told me, be careful about the size of the fish you put into the river. There is no point in filling a river with large fish and then not catching them. Large fish are not good risers, except perhaps to the mayfly, so it is a bad economy to put them in the river and never see them again. In my father's day it took around two years to produce a trout of 2–3 lb. Today I can achieve the same growth rate and weight in one and a half years. Anyway, as I have discovered, the willingness of a trout to rise – whether it be brown or rainbow – depends not on its size, but its age. Younger trout will generally rise more freely and fight harder than older fish but because of their tender age, their mouths are often softer and consequently quite a few are lost in the fight.

I have always contended, though, that size is a relative thing. If I were to be fishing, say, the Upper Test or the Itchen I would be perfectly happy to catch a native brown of around 1 lb; on the Middle Test 2 lb or more would be the target. To me sport does not, or should not, depend on size. Flyfishing for trout is about deception of the fish; size is a very real temptation but it does tend to devalue our sport if a fish is prized because of its size rather than the degree of difficulty experienced in catching it.

VI

THE HOUGHTON TREASURES

FOUNDED in 1822, the Houghton Club was and always will be a fellowship of anglers dedicated to the pursuit of the trout with the fly. It is
therefore part fishing, part social, with members setting as much store by
the good companionship as by the fishing. The rules are few: a club of this
size with only twenty-four members doesn't have the need for too many
rules. One unwritten law, which dates back to the Club's foundation, is that
where possible, members are asked to stay at the Grosvenor Hotel in
Stockbridge and dine in the clubroom every night. This ensures the
preservation of the Club atmosphere as laid down by the founding
members.

The origins of the Houghton Club date back to a chance meeting in 1822
between Canon Beadon and Mr King, the landlord of the Grosvenor Arms –
as the Grosvenor Hotel in Stockbridge was then called – who explained that
the fishing in the parish of Houghton was to let. After a tour of the water,
Canon Beadon, who fished on the Longstock Club's water a mile or so
upstream of Stockbridge, enthusiastically told his close friend Edward
Barnard about his discovery and recommended that he establish a fishing
club on one of the most beautiful stretches of the Middle Test.

Barnard visited the waters, decided Beadon was right and immediately
set about founding the Houghton Fishing Club, offering membership at an
annual subscription of £10 to his acquaintances. That first meeting of the
Club's members under Barnard's secretaryship at Stockbridge comprised
three churchmen: Canon Beadon and the Reverends Henry Dampier and
William Garrett; two Members of Parliament: Henry Warburton and
Charles Taylor; two Knights: Sir James Gardiner and Sir Charles Blois;

William Beckford and Francis L. Beckford Jr; Colonel Walhouse; Francis Popham; and Francis Penn. On that day they also devised the Club's simple rules, one of which showed their concern for the well-being of the Club's keepers:

> Any presents of Fish to persons connected with the Fishery to be borne equally by Members present; it being understood that an Subscriber who shall be present, and who shall not have contributed during the season, shall be first called upon for that purpose.

According to Sir Herbert Maxwell, who edited the first edition of the *Chronicles of the Houghton Fishing Club*, these presents to the keepers were probably designed to compensate them for their low wages, which were little more than retaining fees, with Charles Elton, the Head Keeper earning 14s a week, his underkeeper brother John and James Faithfull receiving 3s and 3s 6d a week respectively.

Unlike today's members, who tend to motor down to Stockbridge from London for a day or two's fishing throughout the season from May to September, those thirteen original members travelled down twice a year: for the hatch of grannom in April and May and again for the emergence of the mayfly in May and June.

It was a biannual pilgrimage with the members travelling down from London as a body – a gathering of friends – by post-chaise and mail coach and staying in Stockbridge for up to three weeks at a time. So they lived together, fished together, ate together and, as a consequence, forged bonds of friendship. These traditions have become the mark of the Houghton Club, the most famous if not the oldest flyfishing club in the world. Fortunately, those original members left behind a permanent reminder of those days, in the form of a number of sketches and lithographs which give some idea of how the 'fishing gents' went about their day's play on the Test. These are contained within the pages of the book in the clubroom on the first floor of the Grosvenor Hotel in Stockbridge.

The book, which is now in its twelfth leather-bound volume, was started not just as a record of the Club, its members, the fish they caught and the flies they used. It is also a fascinating and unique account of the river and its wildlife, of major international events and a history of our 15 miles of the Middle Test, from Leckford and Longstock to the north to Houghton and Horsebridge to the south. Most of all, the book offers an insight into the character and talent of the members from 1822 to the present day. With members tending to stay at the hotel for three weeks at a time, on blowy,

The Houghton Fishing Club at the Grosvenor Hotel, Stockbridge, *c.* 1850

wet and inclement days, when no fly were hatching and no fish were rising, they had plenty of time on their hands. But they were far from idle hands, or idle minds for that matter, because the entries in those early books are a delightful pageant of rhyme, humour, caricature and advice for flyfishermen everywhere.

It is a considerable tribute to present-day members of the Houghton Club that the fellowship of anglers established in 1822 continues to this day. Members today are firm and close friends as were the earlier members at their biannual meetings. In some cases, the Club's membership has comprised fathers and sons, brothers and cousins: the Smith banking family spanned seventy-one years from 1829 to 1900; with Abel, Martin Tucker, Martin Ridley, Sir Gerard, Rupert Oswald, Nigel Martin and Robert L. Newman, who was Martin Ridley Smith's nephew; there have been three Lords of Penryhn from 1845 to 1887; three Normans: George Warde in 1831, Henry in 1842 and Herbert in 1871, the latter two acting as honorary secretaries for an uninterrupted 60 years; Colonel S. Clare and his son Ralph were members when the Club celebrated its centenary in 1922.

I always like to think that those past members who have died, those absent friends who have shared the fishing and the fellowship, are still with us, enjoying the conversation, the humour and friendship of each new generation as it is elected to the Club. As Edward Barnard recorded in the book in 1827:

> Let it be recorded here that in this Club the good example of Izaak Walton our patron saint has been so invariably followed that no jealousy, no envying, no strife, no bickering has ever existed. The wish of the individual, whether expressed or implied has been the law of all, the happiness of each other has been the compass by which all has been steered, no angry word, no selfish feeling has ever betrayed itself in our enviable circle. Every successive meeting has been the means of uniting more firmly, if possible, that good friendship and fellowship that has manifested itself from the beginning, which has been the object of all to encourage, which has been the unalloyed satisfaction of all who have experienced, and which with hearts so constituted it must remain unshaken. Our society may be dissolved by circumstances over which our meeting has established and the remembrance of many happy hours passed in the company of each other can only terminate with our lives.

In his role as honorary secretary, Edward Barnard spent much of his time browbeating and cajoling members to make full use of the book and write about their observations, ideas, or anything else that came to mind about the trout, the fly or the twin passions of most members: eating, and drinking good claret and port. In 1828 he was driven to write:

> This Book has existed since the 16th July 1827; and only a few Members have taken up the Gauntlet thrown down in the opening paper. It is hoped that henceforward both Member and Visitor will exert themselves to increase and improve this joint Stock Property – The wish to overcome their diffidence is the only excuse that can be offered for the unblushing name in which so many of the previous pages have been occupied by the pen of E. Barnard.

There were a number of members willing to pick up such a gauntlet, especially Henry Warburton MP, who is reputed to have written the following verse:

Haste! Haste! Lads of the Hook and Line,
Why are ye lingering? Barnard calls loudly;
Haste! Haste! Charles Elton gives the sign,
His hat decked with Mayflies and wearing it proudly.

Edward Barnard Composing by Francis Grant

Lay aside business, London and cares forget;
Put off engagements for parties and dinners;
Come all Honest Fellows, since here our Club has met,
And leave London enjoyments to Citizen Sinners.

Haste! Haste! Lads of the Hook and Line,
When no selfish feelings, nor jealousies sever;
Friendship's our watchword, Good nature our
    countersign,
Huzza for the Mayfly and Houghton for ever. . . .

Moses is moaning for want of his master
Rose thinks the Colonel uncommonly slack
The Donkey boys had to make Chantrey come faster;
And Faithfull fears Dicky ne'er means to come back

Maton is ready with knives, spoons and dishes,
The Tent rears its 'crest o'er' the meadows so gay;
Old Butt wanders the Gentlemen leaves all the Fishes
To rise ah so freely and still stay away

Haste! Haste! Lads of the Hook and Line

Barnard walks up and down fishing and fretting,
And plans with John Elton the work of each day;
Popham, a sticker at whipping and wetting,
Goes right through each Shallow that comes in his way;
To watch the nice moment when wind and a dark cloud suits
Snow takes his station near some sheltered Bush –
With his plaid Cloak enveloped and pair of stout Water Boots;
Old Watts his attendant, and trusty Bob Lash.

Haste! Haste! Lads of the Hook and Line

What pleasure can vie with the hope and the rapture,
When a trout is well hooked and beginning to flounder!
Except when he proves at the moment of capture
To turn in the scale a thick well-fed three-pounder.
Then oh! 'tis a dainty sight to see the fish at night;
To see Penn in his pockets so warily feeling;
To hear Chantrey uproarious, when he's victorious,
And Garrett who goes to bed every night *reeling*.

Haste! Haste! Lads of the Hook and Line

Oh! What can compare with the joy of a Fisher's Life?
Tranquil, contented, no spleen in his breast;
He finds his amusement each morning a foe to strife
And at night seeks his pillow, with conscience at rest.
With the social companions all his hours pass away,
With fresh air his Health and his spirits increase;
And with heart free from trouble, when he meets his last day
He dies, as he lived, both resigned and in peace.

Haste! Haste! Lads of the Hook and Line

One name that stands out in that roll-call of members, ghillies, keepers and farmers is the artist Sir Francis Chantrey, who joined the Houghton Club in 1824 and took pains to decorate the pages of the book with numerous sketches of his fellow members. Among my personal favourites are his sketch of the Reverend Henry J. Dampier, which bears the inscription:

> Smiling alike, though wind be foul or fair,
> He lights his weed, and puffs away all cares.

Sitting through those long day and night-time hours in the clubroom on bad weather days, he also captured Henry Warburton MP, his top-hat stuck with flies:

> Here to mature his thoughts by deep reflection
> And weigh the argument he'll next debate on
> He kills the Trout, and gives them for dissection
> To the experienced hand of Dr Maton.

Not all of Chantrey's brilliant sketches made it into the pages of the book. It is said that his portrait of Edward Barnard, showing the honorary secretary nursing a glass of port, was one of several. The most agreeable sketch as far as Barnard was concerned was included in the book with a note saying, 'The Best Drawing Chantrey was able to make of Barnard after dinner'.

Not content with filling a number of pages in the book with his artistry, Sir Francis Chantry also designed the trout weather-vane on top of the Town Hall in Stockbridge's High Street.

In addition to these fine examples of Victorian wit and verse, there was a more serious side to the book. Barnard, ever the prodder of conscience, combined his duties as secretary with his undoubted love of fishing the mayfly. But as a Londoner, how could he be certain that when he arrived in Stockbridge the mayfly would be on the water? Simple. . . .

> . . . I selected the plants which were in bloom in the neighbourhood of London as the guide for my departure – and although perhaps an entomologist may consider that it would be more to the purpose to watch the insects, which appear in succession as an index for this purpose – yet so many families of insects feed wholly upon the leaves of plants it is obvious that it is the temperature of the air, which develops the one and gives at the same time existence of the other, which would otherwise perish from the want of food; an emergency against which Nature has wisely provided. . . .

The first flower which gave me notice in the experience of former years, was the Common Garden Tulip – Tulip Gesneriana – which is grown by florists for exhibition in the neighbourhood of London and which being generally, from custom, planted on the 9th November viz Lord Mayor's Day, is so far a good test – and it may be remarked that until all the flowers are fully expanded and the bloom at its height no fear need be entertained by those who remain in London that any time is lost. It is necessary, however, to state that all the tulips grow mainly in flower borders, of which many are of a different and earlier species, must not be mistaked for that now pointed out. . . .

I had at one time hoped that these pages might have been enriched by the instructive pen of him whose ability, acuteness, accuracy and perspicacity stamped a value upon every subject to which he turned his thoughts, which were first attracted to this point by the author of these remarks who now so feebly traces the outline above given – yet this fact is here mentioned as it is conceived that it will add a livelier interest of those Brother Fishermen who now mourn the loss of such a friend to be informed that this subject had been thought worthy of his attention and the first notice of the Elder Flower was the result of his observation.

With reference to insects I believe those who live by the river side will find that the varieties of Dragonfly Libellula precede the Mayfly by a day or two – and the Caperer, Thryganece and the Thorn Fly Liatis nigra will be strong for some days previous upon the waters –

It is not pretended that the foregoing observations are infallible in their indication but they are rather offered in the hope of inducing others to follow the writer in his search for information and to afford him that assistance from the united abilities of his Friends, who he trusts will not disappoint him in the expectation of performance.

So obsessed with mayfly were the Club's members – at a time when free-rising fish were literally there for the taking – that they bought a special tent so that they could dine by the water. It was pitched three miles below the town and was in use from around 1824 until the First World War.

In this tent, promptly at 6.30pm the members would dine and wait for the keepers to call them back to the river for the evening rise. The tent was abandoned after the outbreak of the First World War until 1920 when

. . . a half-hearted attempt was made to revive the old practice, but the tent was found to be in a very rotten state, and beyond repair. It seemed out of the question to buy another, when fast motor cars made it so easy to get to the farthest end of our water in only a few minutes, and so one more pleasant custom has gone west before the march of progress.

The book, however, isn't solely about fishing. As I have said, those members in the early 1800s had plenty of time to write down all kinds of hints and tips on just about anything, and William George Garrett was no exception when he offered his recipe for a hash of venison, beef, mutton, game or wild fowl in 1830.

> One pint more or less of good clear gravy
> One or two onions chopped very very fine
> A little Kyen . . . a little salt
> Two . . . three . . . or four table spoonfuls of Port wine
> Two . . . three . . . or four table spoonfuls of Ketchup

> Make these to boil . . . let the meat be cut very thin
> and be put in when the gravy is boiling . . . turn the
> meat in about one minute . . . stir it or turn it . . . and in
> three minutes let it be taken to the table . . . not to
> stand before eaten . . . as all hashes get hard if allowed
> to stand before eaten.

> Boiled salt beef in clear good gravy with onion
> slices or chopped fine is a dish in high repute.

Barnard tried Garrett's hash of venison and reported:

> Thy hash, Friend Garrett, be it understood,
> Experts crede, I report is good;
> But he who rashly eats the mince for dinner,
> Rises next morning, a repentant sinner.

Barnard's wry, dry sense of humour came into play many times during his years as the Club's honorary secretary. He was particularly taken with Richard Penn's many observations on flyfishing – they are as true now as they were in the 1800s – which were often accompanied by precise pen and ink sketches. As Penn observed: trout tend to lie in

> . . . the confluence of two branches of a stream which has been

divided by a patch of weeds, or that part of a stream which has been narrowed by two weed patches. Fish are also to be found under the bank, opposite to the wind, where they are waiting for the flies which are blown against that bank and fall into the river.

Precise though Penn was in his many dissertations on the way of the trout, one of his more shaky discourses about evening fishing came under Barnard's critical gaze, prompting him to write,

This last is probably an expostfacto observation from having tried the Claret Fly a little too long after dinner.

Barnard signed it: James $\overset{\text{his}}{\underset{\text{mark}}{\times}}$ Faithfull [the Club's Head Keeper]

As Sir Herbert Maxwell revealed in the first edition of the *Chronicles of the Houghton Fishing Club*, members hosted a number of eminent artistic guests, including Sir Edwin Landseer, J. M. W. Turner and Sheridan. They all returned the compliment of their invitation to Stockbridge with such unique flourishes as Landseer's beguiling kitten staring at the goldfish in a bowl in a sketch dated 1832, and Turner's delightful 1849 caricature of a club member.

In lamenting the passing of such illustrations in the book, Sir Herbert Maxwell observed:

It cannot be that the graphic faculty has failed many fishermen, nor has the gentle craft lost favour with artists! No: the fault is with the photographers; the ruthless fidelity of the kodak – the ignoble facility of the snapshot – have sterilised the sketch-book and paralysed the palette in this age when everybody has just caught, is busy catching, or is about to catch a train.

Times were, inexorably, changing. No longer were members travelling down by coach to stay for weeks on end; few had the time to compose amusing anecdotes, carefully constructed rhymes or detailed observations of nature. The Club, too, was under threat in 1874 when they lost three miles of water. As the book recounts:

1874 saw the loss of water from the Machine Barn about half a mile below Stockbridge, down to Bossington: in all, nearly three miles, with the water let to 20 gentlemen who adopted the title of the Houghton Fly Fishing Club. The old Houghton, thus shorn of the ancient territory it had since 1822, retained its headquarters in the Grosvenor Hotel and became known as the Stockbridge Fishing Club.

This situation continued until 1883,

> ...at which time some individual members had bought stretches of water. Gathering in these waters it was decided to form the Stockbridge Fishery Association Ltd in January 1883 with a nominal capital of £20,000.

The original directors of the SFA were Martin R. Smith, Herbert Norman, Alfred Denison, J. Steweart Hodgson and the Earl of Ducie. The situation continued until 1893 when they bought back the water they had lost nineteen years earlier.

As was recorded in the book on New Year's Day 1893:

> This day will be forever memorable in the Club Annals. A lasting debt of gratitude is due those members of the Houghton Club who, at a very critical moment, provided the greater part of the capital necessary for the purchase of our long-lost water. This day we re-enter on the choicest part of the best trout river in England, with the satisfaction of knowing that we are no longer lease-holders. Our work, however, is not yet finished. Further purchases (small in comparison to this) must be made to make our position secure. In taking the fishery over we find the banks in a shameful state of neglect, and the stock of fish very much smaller than when we gave up possession. All this is being carefully remedied.

In the midst of this battle to regain the original Houghton Club waters, my grandfather was made Head Keeper in 1887:

> After more than 40 years' true and devoted service to the Club James Faithfull retired on a well-earned pension, and William Lunn was appointed keeper in his place.

Faithfull died on 26 April 1888 and the book recorded his passing with the line, 'His name was his character.'

A thank you letter from Arthur Rackham to
Mr E. J. Power, 1913

Over the Club's 160-plus years many members have brought guests down to Stockbridge to fish the water, each of whom have made their mark in the book, either in terms of the number of fish caught or in some rhyme or sketch to mark the day. In 1913 Arthur Rackham, the author and illustrator, fished as a guest of Mr Power – who five years earlier had started to teach grandfather how to tie flies. Although Mr Rackham caught only one fish of 1 lb 9oz he obviously enjoyed his three days on the water, sending Mr Power the following letter in July 1913:

My dear Power

Just a line to say how greatly I enjoyed my holiday with you at Stockbridge, and to say how much appreciated were the fish you so kindly sent to my wife. I only wish I had been able to claim them as spoils to my own rod.

But the pleasant days at the river side (almost as pleasant I trust to the inhabitants of the Test as to me) have shed their soothing influence over the past week during the lucid intervals when I have not been correcting proofs.

With very many thanks

Arthur Rackham

One of the Club's more regular guests in the 1900s was H. T. Sheringham, the Fishing Editor of *The Field* who was also responsible for editing Alfred Ronalds's *The Fly-Fisher's Entomology*. It was he that members called upon to write a celebratory poem to honour the Houghton Club's centenary year in 1922.

TO THE HOUGHTON CLUB
IN GRATITUDE

A hundred years beside clear brimming Test,
A hundred years of friendship manifest,
Of Walton's brotherhood and craft professed,
Of bending rods and plunging trout, the best
In all the kingdom, surely ye are blest
Beyond all other anglers! Yet your guest
Mindful of gratitude still unexpressed
Though deep in heart, prays that in future quest
The children's children in the hundredth year
May find the Houghton Club still settled here.
And for himself, when Charon's summons dear
Has thrilled a midnight, he will try to steer
For upper waters straight, not stop to spear
On Styx, or Acheron, or Avernus Mere,
Grim devil-fish or vampires, which men fear
These waters hold: nor pause if dim appear
Shade-fish in misty Lethe: but win clear

> To where blue skies, green grass, bright stream, sun's cheer
> Say 'Here are trout, and here a brimming Test,
> And here a Houghton Club. O happy guest.'

Change, as with nature, has always been a gradual thing for members of the Houghton Club. They were sceptical for many years about adopting the whipping rod and the artificial fly, which on most waters had been in use for twenty years. Many members resisted the change from silk fly lines to the more serviceable and efficient plastic-coated lines for a number of years. And in 1915 after several debates – the last being in 1896 when the motion was defeated by twelve votes to four – the members agreed to allow Sunday fishing on the Houghton Club waters.

During the First World War most of the members were busy with war work of one kind and another, so very few of them attended the Club. But as their contributiuon to the war effort, they did allow Army officers in the area to fish the water as guests of the Club. On one such day the secretary reported:

> Guns in Flanders distinctly audible in the evening, after the wind dropped. General Baden Powell confirms this statement.

The Great War, as it was termed, was a terrible conflict claiming many of the valley's young men. No wonder that when the Peace Treaty between England and Germany was signed on 4 June 1919 the book recorded the fact that 'the town crier, clad in a top hat and a Union Jack, was busy announcing the good news in Stockbridge at frequent intervals during the afternoon.' And in full view of the many members down one month later in that year of celebration: 'Peace celebrations are held in the town. An effigy of the Kaiser was burnt in front of the hotel at night, by way of a climax.'

The First World War also witnessed the first recorded fish taken on the Houghton Club waters by a lady fisher, when Lady Sophie Scott took five trout weighing 10 lb 2oz from Park Stream on 13 July 1916.

Lady guests of the Houghton Club have fished regularly ever since, although I doubt whether I will ever see lady members admitted to the Club in my lifetime.

In 1932, after a long illness, grandfather retired and my father took over as Head Keeper of the Houghton Club waters. The book reports:

> Lunn, after over forty years service to the Club has retired as, although he is better, is unfit for further active work and is to receive

a pension. After Lunn his son is being promoted in his father's place.

The Thirties were a busy time for many Club members, who actively fought against the metalling of the roads from Stockbridge down the valley to Bossington. They lost, but only after a hard-fought public enquiry which lasted many months. But as the decade drew on there were other more pressing matters occupying the members' attention.

War was in the air, and when the Army moved to Stockbridge for manoeuvres, the clubroom was handed over to them and officers were invited to fish the Houghton Club's waters.

Then, on 3 September 1939 the book reported:

P.M. announced state of war at 11.15. Fish as depressed as fishermen and did not rise by day.

The news did not improve as this note on 10 May 1940 shows:

Germany today invaded Holland and Belgium, Mr Neville Chamberlain resigned and Mr Winston Churchill became P.M. A warm bright day with a poor rise. Few fish moving.

As a consequence of the Second World War the Club was reduced to a skeleton staff – 'and it was decided that no new work should be undertaken that was not absolutely essential' – and the fish stocks were reduced, with many trout sold off to the Army Catering Corps. Bombing in London also prevented members freeing themselves from that war-ravaged city to spend a few days of peace by the Test. As was recorded in 1940:

Petrol restrictions and war work prevented too many members attending and the railway service was very bad. A bomb on 9 September did considerable damage to the line outside Waterloo and for some weeks no trains could go further than Clapham Common. This also prevented the movement of live eels from the Houghton Club waters. At the London market eels were fetching 1s 10d per lb.

Despite their generosity to the services, the Club's relations with the Army were not always good. As the secretary reported in 1940:

In the autumn some Australian troops arrived in Sheepbridge and proceeded to bomb the water. They did not kill very much and fortunately they were shortly afterwards transferred to other fields – perhaps to Libya where no doubt they put their bombs to better use.

In 1944, however, the brave action of a Spitfire pilot brought good cheer to Club members:

A Spitfire pilot Squadron Leader O'Brien DFC, operating from Wallop, brought down a Junkers 88 which crashed in flames just off the Stockbridge–King's Somborne Road. This happened about 2pm in view of many.

A year later, on 8 May 1945, the war was over and those members in Stockbridge reported:

This day is declared to be V.E. Day for the end of the war in Europe, and a general holiday with all shops closed, the same for tomorrow, and no letters or telegrams can be sent before the day after that. One pleasing feature of the holidays is that Mr Pryor having no business to attend to in London is able to stay for an extra day on the river.

As with any gathering of friends at that time, the mood in the clubroom was at times quite frivolous, as one member wrote in 1945 after two days of sparse rises and few fish caught:

Any depression ... was much relieved by a most kind present from Mr Stephenson of five bottles of Crofts 1927 and four of Rudesheim, which were all consumed and greatly appreciated at the 'High Tea'!

My grandfather died on 10 June 1942 and the book is filled with tributes and obituaries. Three years later my grandmother died and the secretary recorded:

Alfred Lunn's mother died and was buried at the cemetery in Romsey. She was married to William Lunn in 1894 and proved to be an excellent wife for him, as she took a great deal of interest in his experiments and did a lot of writing for him, for which he had not been much educated. From 1894 until William Lunn's retirement in

1932 there was always a hearty welcome for any member who liked to go to their house for tea and her apple jelly became quite famous. The members who can go back far enough must have the most happy recollections of those happy days.

On his retirement they took a house at Baddesley on the high ground above Romsey where she now lies in the next grave to William in the cemetery. At her death she was in her 81st year.

So we come to more modern times. Although present-day members of the Houghton Club are busy working men who motor down to Stockbridge through the season and stay for less time than the Club's founding fathers, some have picked up Barnard's gauntlet and in fine style continued the traditions of filling the book with their humour and observations. Among my favourites is Colonel Pryor's poem to the rainbow trout. The first record of rainbows entering our waters was in 1896 when Mr Herbert Norman presented the Club with four hundred yearlings. Three years later, Sir John Gladstone took two rainbows of 1 lb 15oz and 1 lb 2oz. But the debate as to whether they should be stocked in the hallowed waters of the Houghton Club raged for some six years, until in 1949 my father was given permission to stock them in earnest. But there were still some dissenters, notably Sir Eastman Bell, the Club's honorary secretary, which prompted Colonel Pryor to pen the following verse in 1954:

RAINBOW

Why should our members grouse about
That splendid fish the Rainbow trout
To me, for all it's little whims
It is the noblest fish that swims
I know it wanders quite a bit
But why the Devil shouldn't it?
Cruising for instance, up the Bends
To see the World, and meet its friends
Making at times a playful rise
It gives the members exercise
If, when in true olympic style
You've chased it over half a mile
It makes a sudden homeward tack
Or rises just behind your back

Then hurries off to base again,
You've had your fun – so why complain?

Hunting a quarry of that sort
Is not a sedentary sport.
I know the purists always frown
On any trout that isn't brown
And furthermore go on to say
In their authoritative way
(which means of course you wouldn't know
You silly ignorant, so and so)
'It's not a trout it's just a char'
That shows what purists really are
For called by any other name
It's just as beautiful and game
It feeds (on nothing) all day long
Nor waits for any dinner gong
Whereas its cousin Fario
Its nose will very seldom show
Till stimulated by a rise
Of different sorts of water flies,

To show how people's views can vary
Our honorary secretary
Who personally was known as quite
A violent anti Rainbowite
Or never to have cast a fly
That wasn't absolutely dry
Yesterday found his iron will
Defeated by the lust to kill
And with a nymph, well under water
Achieved a pretty wholesale slaughter.
So let us hope, at last that this is
The end of both his prejudices
And that last evening he came back
(With six large Rainbows in a sack)
A Nympho-Rainbow-Maniac.

VII

THE FISHING GENTS

A SPECIAL treat for me as a boy was to return home from school towards the end of May or the beginning of June, during the annual mayfly hatch, to find fishing rods resting against the garden hedge. This meant the 'gents', as my grandfather and father called them, who had been angling on the nearby Beats, had stopped by for tea. The daytime hatch was over and the early evening fall of spent mayfly had not yet started. These are the dead and dying males and the egg-laying females, which die exhausted immediately after their job is done.

My father would be standing at the back door, keeping an eye on the river for the first signs of the fall of spent mayfly and I would go into Riverside Cottage and take a peek round the scullery door at the men in the front room. Most days there would be at least three members of the Houghton Club relaxing in the armchairs. They looked awfully grand to me, and their talk was of things I seldom understood, until the conversation turned to the river and its fly life and trout.

These teas were a daily ritual throughout the season, particularly during mayfly when most of the members of the Club came down to fish at least once. They were started by my grandmother and continued by my mother but over the years the menu never changed: thin slices of bread and butter and homemade apple jelly, followed by a slice of fruit cake. On such occasions mother always gave the front room an extra dusting and cleaning, and in the hallway she always filled the basin in the marble-topped washstand with fresh warm water so that the gents could wash their hands before tea.

At this special time when the fishing gents came for tea, the glass on the

95

front of grandfather's two large showcases on either side of the fireplace was given an extra clean so that their contents were shown off to their very best. Inside these cases were the stuffed animals and birds grandfather had collected, trapped or shot, arranged in natural settings by one of his many friends, to make a fine-looking display. Among others, I remember a bittern, a kingfisher, a dabchick, a goosander, an otter, a heron and two small ring doves.

What impressed me most about these occasions was the heady, expensive aroma of Havana cigars; a scented haze that hung over the room long after the gents had returned to the water. It seemed to give the front room a touch of class.

Mother was well-pleased after these teas, particularly when she found half a crown – which was worth a lot in those days – under one of the plates as a reward for the tea. Sadly, those days have long gone; members now drive themselves back to the Grosvenor Hotel for a cuppa.

What I didn't know as a child was that those fishing gentlemen moulded my life, not least because they were members of the Houghton Club who employed my grandfather and father. More importantly, as I later discovered, if it hadn't been for one of these gents the Lunn dynasty at the Houghton Club – three uninterrupted generations of riverkeepers, spanning more than a century – would not have been established in 1887 by my grandfather.

He was born of humble, working class origins in London, the eldest of five children, three of whom died of smallpox. He, too, had smallpox when he was three, but recovered. His father was killed at sea so his mother, my great grandmother, with one child and another expected, was forced to move back to her father's home. He managed a brickyard in Newport, near Saffron Walden, Essex, and grandfather went there as a labourer at the tender age of seven, working from 4am to 8pm for two shillings a week.

Then education was not compulsory, or free, but grandfather educated himself sufficiently. With the help of a woman who kept a night-school near where he lived in Newport, he passed the entrance exam to the local grammar school at the age of seven. However, his uncle, who had succeeded his grandfather as manager of the brickyard, prevented him from attending the school because, as Waller Hills writes in his book *River Keeper*:

> He would neither forgo the two shillings a week that Lunn earned, nor would he find the money to buy the necessary school-books.

So my grandfather went back to the 16-hour-a-day grind of making bricks. At night he was often so exhausted that he would fall asleep where he was without changing his clothes. In the daytime he was treated unkindly and often beaten cruelly.

When he was twelve he ran away from this slavery and took a job on a farm. Two years later, the gamekeeper at High Ashurst, near Box Hill, Surrey, took grandfather on as a keeper's boy, making him responsible for wiring rabbits, rearing pheasant and trapping vermin. Between the ages of sixteen and twenty he was one of the ten gardeners at High Ashurst. In 1882 the gardening staff was reduced, so grandfather took a keepering job with Sir Arthur Clay at Burrows Lea, near Shere in Surrey. It was there that he met Mr Herbert Norman, who at the time was secretary of the Houghton Club. Over the years grandfather must have impressed Mr Norman, because in 1886, four years after their first meeting, he was invited to join him as his personal attendant on the Test at Stockbridge. After a tour of the water grandfather happily accepted the job of Head Keeper, taking on the Houghton Club waters at the age of twenty-four.

Grandfather retired in 1931 after forty-four years as Head Keeper. He handed over to my father, who on his retirement at the end of 1962, passed responsibility for the Houghton Club waters down to me.

As a child, I was brought up to believe that the fishing gents who sat in the front room and took tea were akin to gods: it was an upstairs-downstairs, them-and-us situation which involved considerable mutual respect. It worked perfectly, with no one side taking advantage of the other. But it was only on my first sortie to the river in 1934 with Dr Ivan Magill – carrying his net and bag, occasionally playing a fish or two, and receiving a box of chocolates as my reward – that I came into close contact with these gods. Sir Harold Gillies also took quite a shine to me, and I learned a lot about the fly and the trout and its capture during those long summer afternoons with him. I also have cause to be very grateful to Sir Eastman Bell and Mr T. Murray Sowerby, who paid my school fees.

When I was a lad many of the Houghton Club members had regular ghillies, chosen from the local village men of Houghton and Stockbridge. Each would appear on duty when 'his' gentleman came down to fish. Others, however, used their chauffeurs to double as ghillies and, more often than not, the resident experts William and Alfred Lunn were also in attendance.

Some of those regular ghillies were a law unto themselves. One in particular, named Vince, was a favourite of A. N. Gilbey. Vince was very loyal, but didn't take kindly to a reprimand if he netted a fish badly or was

Grandfather with A. N. Gilbey and his ghillie, Vince

slow to come to Gilbey's aid.

One of the best of many stories about this odd couple, village man and aristocrat, was the day when Vince flicked a horsefly from Mr Gilbey's cheek. Gilbey asked him what it was and then enquired, 'And what do they do?'

'A horsefly, Sir, spends most of its time on the arse of a horse,' Vince explained.

'Are you telling me my face looks like a horse's arse?' replied Gilbey.

'No, Sir,' said Vince, 'but those flies aren't easily fooled.'

Mr Gilbey was a hard fisher, a man who would never miss an opportunity to cast at and catch a rising fish, so much so that he would often break off in mid-sandwich if he spotted a trout rising nearby. On a day that lives on in the Houghton Club's records, Mr Gilbey and Vince were lunching at Sheepbridge Shallows when a fish rose some three parts of the way across the river beyond them.

So the story goes, Mr Gilbey dropped his sandwich and waded into the river to get below the rising fish, calling back to Vince to bring him another

Looking upstream from Cooper's Meadow and Stockbridge

The Clubroom of the Houghton Fishing Club at the Grosvenor Hotel, Stockbridge

glass of port. Once in position, he realised that he needed to 'pump ship', as he always described it, and while relieving himself he also decided to change his fly. Vince was halfway towards him when the angler remembered he didn't have a landing net. Gilbey knew Vince too well to tempt fate and waited until the ghillie had delivered his glass of port before sending him back for the net. As he said later that night in the clubroom, Vince had drunk enough of his port over the years.

Lord Harmsworth, the Liberal MP and the younger brother of the newspaper magnate Lord Northcliffe, was a revered member of the Houghton Club from 1925 until his death in 1948. He favoured a ghillie named Mr Fudge, a well turned-out and competent assistant who was also a special constable in the village. When Mr Fudge was not available to accompany his lordship because of his police duties, I was called upon to take his place.

His lordship was a wry, softly-spoken gentleman and a good angler of his day, but he liked his snooze after lunch and spreading his ample body on his mackintosh laid out on the bank he would bed down in the afternoon sunshine. His instruction to me, on that first occasion I went out with him, was that I should wake him up if a good trout rose. I was petrified to do any such thing, preferring to 'do a Fudge' by keeping the flies off his lordship's face so as not to disturb him. One thing I didn't want to be responsible for was waking up the great man, only for him to hook a rising fish and discover it was merely a grayling.

E. H. Elles was a kindly member of the Houghton Club whose chauffeur, Redman, doubled as his ghillie. Harry Redman and 'the Guv'nor', as Redman called his master, got on famously and many's the time I went down to the water with them. The fact that I was only just out of school seemed to bring out the schoolboy in Harry Redman. I remember one occasion at the water's edge when I'd be trying my damnedest to steer Mr Elles towards a good fish, when Redman managed to divert his master's attention by throwing a small stone into the river. Excitedly indicating the spreading ring on the water he shouted, 'There, Sir, that looked like a good fish'.

T. Murray Sowerby was another gentle and patient fisher. On my first day at the water with him, he left me with his rod and tackle so I could try to catch a fish while he collected his brother from the station. I am sorry to say he returned to find me up an apple tree trying to extricate his fly which, complete with cast, had wrapped itself round one of the upper branches.

One of Mr Sowerby's claims to fame in the Houghton Club was the kind of fishing story so far-fetched that anyone would be reluctant to tell it.

He was, he said, fishing the Mill Beat with a Houghton Ruby on his cast, which he offered to a good fish rising upstream. It took the fly, Mr Sowerby struck too hard and the trout escaped.

Retrieving his line, he tied on another Ruby and sat down on a bench to watch for another fish. Sure enough, another trout rose, prompting Mr Sowerby to kneel and flick a shortish line over the bank canopy to put his fly over the fish. It rose, Mr Sowerby struck, felt the fish, but had the cast minus its fly spring back towards him. This was to happen a third time 50 yards upstream. He decided there had to be something wrong with his cast, so he changed it, tied on a new point and a fourth Houghton Ruby; surely this time he would get a fish in the net?

Moving up, he spotted a trout rising consistently in midstream, opposite a tall comfrey plant. Then the fish sipped down another natural fly a little further upstream. Mr Sowerby cast his fly a couple of feet beyond where the fish had last risen, assuming that it was taking fly as it made its majestic progress upstream. The trout rose, Mr Sowerby struck, and after a short battle the fish was safely netted; in its jaw were four Houghton Rubies!

Colonel W. A. Pryor, another great fisher, was well-known for his ability to catch a large number of fish and always seemed able to catch every fish he saw. He used to shoot with a Mr Allington, a gentleman farmer from Bedfordshire who always carried a Majestic potato around in his pocket because he believed it kept rheumatism away.

On one of the days I went out with Mr Allington he climbed out of the car, lengthened his cast and started chucking his fly on the water. I asked him if he had seen a trout rise, because I hadn't seen any movement at all. He turned while in mid-cast and snorted, 'There's no need to see a fish, Mick, there's hundreds of 'em in here.'

One day Mr Allington took me on one side and said, 'I think Colonel Pryor tells lies, Lunn. You know, he told me he saw six fish and he caught six fish, and I don't believe it.'

My father didn't believe this story either, especially after one evening when he went out with the Colonel. On this occasion, the Colonel hooked and lost a good fish during the evening rise, leaving the Ginger Quill in its jaw. Later, on the way back to the car, father saw a fish rising where the earlier trout had been lost. He offered the Colonel a Sedge and watched as the fly was duly cast to the fish. The trout rose and took the Sedge, but during the fight it broke free. The line was reeled in and father ran his fingers down the cast to dry and re-anoint the fly, only to find it linked, hook to hook, with a Ginger Quill.

Colonel Pryor was a noted roamer who suffered no qualms when he caught a fish on another member's Beat. When walking back to the Grosvenor Hotel he just couldn't resist casting to any rising fish he saw, wherever it was. He made no secret of it, and members expected and respected his 'poaching' with easy good humour. He subsequently wrote an ode on the subject, which went,

> Of food and wine I've had my fill,
> I think I'll wander to the Mill,
> And if it's all the same to you
> I shall fish on Attwoods, too.

His other entries in the book in the clubroom were equally entertaining, including his masterpiece to the Sherry Spinner,

ODE TO A SHERRY SPINNER

> Outside the Grosvenor after dinner
> I met a female sherry spinner
> I watched her as she hurried by
> Shimmering against the evening sky
> Clutching between her two hind legs
> a pearly sac containing eggs
> And saw her dump her precious load
> Well in the centre of the road
> 'Poor Soul,' I thought, 'If soul you've got
> Why did you make so rash a shot?
> Did you mistake some treacherous gleam
> for Test's more hospitable stream?
> Or did you, Lady, reason thus?
> Dear George dislikes expense and fuss
> I'll leave my darlings to their fates
> Planted upon the Stockbridge rates.'
> Lady, if so, I doubt if that's
> The proper way to treat one's brats.

Sir Eastman Bell, a bachelor and a keen angler, was a very superstitious man who loathed to be wished good luck before setting off for his chosen Beat. In fact, he was always overjoyed if someone wished him bad luck. My father tells the story of how two elderly ladies watched as Sir Eastman played a fish, and called out, 'Oh, you are having some good luck'. The fish immediately got off and Sir Eastman raised his hat.

Like some of the Houghton Club's evening trout, Sir Eastman was also a late riser and generally missed the draw for Beats in the clubroom after breakfast. That was never a problem, because members always put him down for Upper Park Stream. It was always his favourite place on the river, a Beat where he did well with rod and line.

There are few places on our stretch of the Test which I can pass without a story springing to mind: episodes I was involved in myself, or anecdotes passed from one Lunn generation to the next.

Just about every Beat on the Houghton Club water has a hut, bush, bridge or place on the bank named after a past or present member. These either signify a generous gift to the Club or mark an amusing or important personal event. Chantrey has his Corner, Popham has his Pollard and Norman has his Bush. Henry Warburton MP, one of the Club's original thirteen members, has his Wash, which is just at the head of Radnor's Island. It was here that he was 'taken short', as Edward Barnard, the Club's secretary at the time, recorded in the book on 3 June 1831.

Not too far upstream of Warburton's Wash lies Poacher's Point, one of two places on the Butts Larder Beat where the fish under the far bank can be reached. It is also the only place on the river where the Club shares the water, because the opposite bank belongs to the Marshcourt Estate, once owned by Mr Herbert Johnson.

It was at Poacher's Point that father overheard a conversation between two fishermen: one on Marshcourt, the other a Houghton Club member on the opposite bank. Sadly, both men were hard of hearing which often meant that their conversations could be clearly heard, even if they were the length of a cricket pitch away. As father tells it, this shouted conversation began with one angler saying, 'Morning, did you hear about my loss?'

'Was it a big 'un?' called back the other, thinking that the angler was referring to a monster trout.

'Yes,' said the Marshcourt angler, 'it was the wife.'

The Wells Hut on The Bends, which is one of our topmost Beats, was presented to the Club by C. M. Wells. It was here, while sheltering from a thunderstorm, that the two long-serving members, Captain H. D. Sowerby and Colonel W. M. Pryor, decided to have an early lunch and sit out the storm. During lunch they tossed the occasional crust of bread into the flowing waters outside the hut door. It wasn't long before they heard a series of rushes and splashes coming from under the cattle bridge just downstream from the hut. The Colonel looked at the Captain, and in minutes they had wrapped a piece of bread crust around a large Orange and Partridge Nymph and started to drift it downstream to the feeding trout. The bread passed over the trout, the trout rose and the Captain played it towards the Colonel's waiting net. But the happy ending wasn't to be: the fish lunged between the posts on the bridge and broke the cast.

'Try again,' said the Colonel, 'I believe there were two fish there.'

Having run out of bread crusts, they fastened a piece of Cheddar cheese round a fly. The Captain cast it further downstream just as a peal of thunder shook the ground at their feet and stair-rods of rain slanted from the sky. The Captain dropped his rod on the bank and the pair made for the shelter of the hut. When the shower stopped the Captain returned to his fishing rod to find that he'd got a fish on it. After playing it for several minutes, he managed to get it close enough to the bank to discover that his fish was a large eel. After a twisting fight, the Colonel netted the eel up onto the concrete parapet outside the hut, unhooked the fly and started to hit the poor thing hard enough to kill it.

The Captain was interrupted by another downpour, which drove them both back into the hut. When they emerged after five minutes, the eel had managed to get back into the river.

Half an hour later the Colonel spotted a fish rising upstream in mid-river. Returning to more orthodox methods, the Captain tied a Brown Upright on his cast and moved up to address the rising trout. On his second cast, the fish – which had been taking the olives hatching after the summer thunderstorm – rose to the artificial and was firmly hooked. After a short fight, the fish was netted by the Colonel and pulled up onto the bank. It was, they both agreed, a worthy opponent: a superb 4 lb brown trout with a Brown Upright in one side of its jaw, a bread crust wrapped around a large Orange and Partridge Nymph in the other side.

One of the nicest illustrated books I have ever seen of the southern chalkstreams, particularly our water, is E. A. Barton's *An Album of the Chalk Streams*, which was published in 1946. I was a boy just out of school, doing my first year's apprenticeship as a riverkeeper, when I met Dr Barton. He was a kindly man and a good angler, but I didn't at first recognise these qualities. On our first meeting I was designated his 'packhorse', the lad who carried his heavy tripod and plate camera in addition to his fishing tackle.

Looking at his photographs from those days, I have to admit he was a great photographer: an artist with the ability to 'paint with light'. Whether he captured the sun burning through the dawn mist, the noontime glare and flat calm of a cloudless June day, or the evening rise under a setting sun, his photographs are one of the few reminders in print of my early days on the Houghton Club waters.

The doctor's performance as a photographer was always a source of great amusement to me as a teenager. After a lot of walking up and down and muttering to himself, he would instruct me to place the camera in a specific position on the bank and then place myself in 'the frame', meaning in the centre of the picture. He would then spend a lot of time fiddling with the focus and the tripod legs, occasionally diving under the black sheet while composing his picture. After this palaver we would swap places: him in the picture, me clutching the rubber, bulb-shaped shutter release. The result would be a picture of the good doctor as expert flyfisher, often with his rod bent double as if a deep-bellied Houghton Club trout was on the end of his line. More often than not, though, the 'trout' was a brick tied on the line.

On one rare occasion the good doctor decided to frame his picture around a 'young flyfisher' under the big poplars above Black Bridge. He said this was, 'in order to emphasise the immense contrast in size' between man and nature. If you're lucky enough to own a copy of Barton's splendid photographic album of our chalkstreams in their prime, that's me on page 27.

As a flyfisher, Dr Barton was one of life's 'naturals', though he did insist on greasing his fly line with deer's fat. As an ardent follower of G. E. M. Skues – the man who introduced nymph fishing as a branch of our sport – Dr Barton always favoured fishing with Skues's Little Red Sedge. Often, when out with him on the water, I'd follow my father's advice, 'If you find a fish that is asking to be caught, nip off his Sedge under some pretence and pop on a Lunn's Particular.'

I managed this on several occasions, and when he asked me why I had changed his fly I would tell him that the fish he had cast to and hooked was, 'rising to spent fly'. He believed me every time, and caught a lot of fish as a result.

One of the fishing gents I fished with regularly over a period of twenty years, was the Honourable Lewis Douglas, the American Ambassador from 1947 to 1950. As a 'fishing ambassador', he was given honorary membership of the Houghton Club; he later persuaded the Club to give him full membership, and to this day he is the only American citizen ever to be elected to the Club's rolls.

He was a charming man and a good angler who always fished with what he called his 'trusty Garrison' cane rod and greased silk fly line. He was also responsible for bringing the Grey Wulff and Rat Faced McDougall fly patterns – which are much favoured in the United States – to the Houghton Club waters.

My first modelling job, at 16, when E. A. Barton photographed me *Below the Big Poplars* for his chalkstream album

Sadly, Mr Douglas lost an eye when fishing for salmon on the lower reaches of the Test around Nursling. Apparently, it was a very windy day and as he retrieved his fly it touched a piece of weed and came hurtling back to him, catching him in the eye. This didn't deter him, and he was back with us a year later, none of his fly-catching abilities impaired by the loss of sight in one eye.

Sometimes he and I would stop for lunch and I would ask his permission to listen to the cricket commentary on the car radio. At this he always chuckled quietly to himself, then asked me what a 'square leg', 'long leg' and 'silly mid-on' were all about.

One of my father's favourite non-fishing stories about the gents concerns an anonymous young guest.

In the Thirties the Grosvenor Hotel was a very austere place; there were chamberpots under every bed, as opposed to the en suite bathrooms of today. There were also a number of pretty young chambermaids on the staff, and one evening after dinner the young guest was told that he should order early morning tea in his room because the chambermaid who brought it was 'a real smasher'. He duly ordered early morning tea at 7am, rising at 6am to bathe, shave and get back into bed to await the chinking china. On the stroke of seven there came a knock on the door and there in the open doorway stood the hunched figure of a man in his seventies in a green beize apron, holding a tray laden with tea and toast.

'Where's the chambermaid?' demanded the young guest.

'I don't know', replied the old retainer, 'but the teapot comes from Staffordshire.'

I have always said that longevity and fishing go together and when asked why, I always point to C. M. Wells, the Eton schoolmaster, Greek scholar and cricketer who played for both Surrey and Middlesex. In 1899 while playing for Middlesex he scored 246 off the Nottinghamshire bowlers and in the same innings took nine wickets. He caught his last trout on the Houghton Club waters when he was in his ninety-second year. He was also a great authority on wine, and I can remember times in the clubroom when he not only named the vintage of a particular wine, but also the vineyard it came from.

I went with him to the river on many occasions. Besides catching fish I enjoyed watching the river or listening to his experiences of fishing for salmon in Norway. He had a great reputation for the very large fish he took off the Bolstad River, many of which weighed anything from a 20 lb 'tiddler' to a monstrous 65-pounder. I also listened to his cricketing exploits with interest and amusement and if I really managed to get him going he would readily get up off the seat and show me how to deliver a chinaman or a googly: three steps down the bank and over came the hand. 'Remember, Mick,' he would always say, 'let the ball out of the back of your hand . . . like this, do you see?'

Although there was always something of a them-and-us situation between my grandfather and father and members of the Houghton Club, the same is not true today. Ever since I was a lad I've been known as 'Mick', not 'Lunn'. Consequently, many members have been and have become great friends as well as employers.

One such friend was Sir Laurence Dunne, the Chief Metropolitan Magistrate, who I always fished with when he was down in Stockbridge. He was a fine man and eager to learn everything he could about the river, its fly, wildlife and surrounding vegetation. This was so much so that through the winter months I would often visit him at his home in Sunninghill, near Ascot.

There in his drawing room on crisp Sunday mornings I would show him how to tie a Hackle Bluewing, which represented the hatching blue winged olive, then he would have a go. On other days he would take me through his diary, which listed every fish he caught and every stag or pheasant he ever shot. He loved keeping diaries and we would spend many hours together writing up our observations from the previous season. He also used to help me out with my after-dinner speeches – something I have been invited to do since I took over as Head Keeper – telling me stories and anecdotes that enlivened my performance greatly.

N. Bengough was a man who always admitted that he was an average fisher who never expected great things, but was thrilled when everything went right and he caught a full bag. He and Sir Laurence Dunne were close friends and Sir Laurence, the expert, was constantly trying to pass on his know-how to Mr Bengough, who was a constant and attentive protégé. The two men were great jokers and their leg-pulling and laughter were typical of the spirit of the Houghton Club.

One such cause for merriment came about when Sir Laurence persuaded Mr Bengough to tie up his own flies, giving him a few lessons on the clubroom table. Sure enough, Mr Bengough arrived in the clubroom after breakfast one May morning and proudly showed Sir Laurence a very large furry object tied to a hook.

'What's that supposed to be, Ben?' asked Sir Laurence, turning the fly between his forefinger and thumb.

'A Mayfly, Laurie,' replied Mr Bengough, 'I tied it up this morning.'

Taking a Mayfly from his own aluminium fly box, Sir Laurence dropped it in Mr Bengough's hand and said, 'No, Ben, this is a Mayfly. You're not seriously suggesting that you cast that bally thing on the River Test, are you?'

Mr Bengough set off for his Beat, his tail between his legs, but, many hours later, returned to the clubroom for dinner, his face flushed and excited. As he came through the door Sir Laurence boomed, 'Did you put that dreadful concoction of yours on the water, Ben?'

'Yes,' said Mr Bengough, pouring himself a whisky and soda, 'and it was paid quite a compliment.'

'And what was that?' smiled Sir Laurence.

'Well,' replied Mr Bengough, 'it not only took five good fish, but one of those naturals came down and rogered it.'

There wasn't a dry eye in the room.

On another evening, I was fishing with Mr Bengough, who had bagged nine fish and we were searching for a tenth to complete his bag. Sir Laurence had only taken two brace and as we passed him Mr Bengough remarked, very loudly, 'One more fish, Mick, and we can go off to the cinema.'

Mr Bengough was something of a tartar when it came to netting a fish, mostly because he had been told by 'the experts' that he had to keep level with his fish during the fight. When it came to the larger, friskier Houghton Club trout this could mean a great deal of walking up and down. On one occasion I bent down to net a trout that had pretty well given up the fight, only to find Mr Bengough had walked the fish downstream five paces. Down again I went, but no, he had moved even further downstream, intent as he was on staying level with the exhausted fish as it was carried by the current.

After three more attempts to net the fish Mr Bengough casually asked: 'Where do you want to net him, Mick?'

'How about Romsey, sir?' I replied, more than a little sarcastically, Romsey being a town some 10 miles away.

Mr Bengough also had a habit of falling in the river rather often. This meant that if there were deep puddles of water on the fish room floor at the Grosvenor Hotel the member responsible was described as having 'done a Bengough'.

His response was always to explain that it wasn't that he was awkard, he was simply more adventurous than most. Adventurous or not, I was with him at the water one afternoon and persuaded him to kneel when casting to a fish so that we could get closer to our target in an attempt to avoid the fly dragging on the current. The fish rose, he struck, hooked the fish and went to stand up, faltering as he did, and fell face down into the river. He surfaced a second or two later, his hat still perched on his head and a broad grin spreading across his face as he lifted his rod high, the trout still firmly held by the hook.

He was a delightful man, one who always told me that the fishing and Stockbridge were what kept him alive.

Sir Harold Gillies, the pioneer plastic surgeon who did so much to help those who suffered horrific burns during the Second World War, was also a scratch golfer, a reasonable artist, a joker, a fine angler, and something of an eccentric: spending the whole of one evening at a cocktail party wearing a false nose. One of his great obsessions was finding new angles on angling, so to speak. He was the only member I knew who pitched a tent on the banks of the Houghton Club's waters and slept there the night so that he could wake up and fish the dawn rise.

One of his many experiments concerned the way in which a gut cast would break so easily, particularly when striking a fish. It was after considerable thought that he came up with the idea of tying an elastic band between the line and the cast as a sort of shock-absorber.

His first trial with this invention took place one June afternoon. His cast to a rising fish was a bit on the heavy side, but for some reason the fish obligingly took his fly. To say that the elastic band stretched is something of an understatement, but fortunately it didn't break and we managed to net the fish. 'Obviously,' he remarked, turning to me, 'a thicker piece of elastic is called for, Mick.'

'But,' I replied, 'that would make the cast land even more heavily, Sir Harold.'

He snorted contemptuously and abandoned the idea. It is interesting to note, though, that some forty years later an enterprising company did market a similar device called Shock Gum, which I'm told is used by many stillwater flyfishers.

Sir Harold was taken with stories about Colonel Peter Hawker, the early nineteenth century sportsman who used to fish from horseback when he was on the Test at Longparish. Not to be outdone, Sir Harold instructed me to take the wheel of his Bentley and drive it as close as I dare to the bank at Cooper's Meadow, while he stood on the passenger seat, head and shoulders out through the sunshine roof, casting his fly upon the water. He did rise one fish, but generally we put every trout down for miles.

Realising that I was getting more than a little cross, he instructed me to park, telling me we would walk up. He was soon into a fish, but instead of playing it in the time-honoured, rod-up manner, he lowered his rod tip and wound and wound until the trout was almost nudging the top ring. Realising that we were facing a disaster, I quickly pulled up my waders and whipped the fish out on to the bank, really annoying Sir Harold, who had had yet another of his experiments foiled.

Like Colonel Pryor, Sir Harold was always one of the last to go down to the river and always one of the last to return to the clubroom. One July day he went off in pursuit of grayling and caught fourteen. On returning to the fish room at the Grosvenor Hotel, he had me thread them on a long piece of string, 18in. apart. He then tied the string and the fish around his waist and proceeded on upstairs to the clubroom, circling the dinner table where the other members were eating, saying 'I've just had a day with the grayling'. He continued to circle the table and then left the room, to the raucous laughter of the members present.

Sir Harold was also something of a practical joker. After fishing during the day, members' lines would be dried and greased on the lawn outside the fish room in readiness for the evening rise. On more than one occasion, Sir Harold took great delight in sneaking out before members came down to thread one of the lines through the nearby lavatory window, attaching the end to the toilet roll.

Despite his eccentricities, Sir Harold was a very fine angler, a person from whom I learned a great deal.

Sir Ivan Magill, the anaesthetist, joined the Houghton Club in 1931 and was a great friend of Sir Harold Gillies. In 1968 he celebrated his eightieth birthday in the clubroom and during the evening, over port, he was asked which was his greatest achievement: the 5 lb brown he had landed that afternoon or his invention of the Magill Tube.

Sir Ivan was more than a little deaf and given to nodding off, sometimes in mid-sentence, so the question was asked again. Stirring slightly, Sir Ivan looked up, a twinkle in his eye and said: 'Well, dear boy, I think my finest achievement was the night sister at the Westminster Hospital.'

VIII

THE ENEMIES WITHIN

OVER the three generations that my family has been keepering the Houghton Club waters much has gradually changed, and mostly for the worse: an example of man's inhumanity to nature.

Memory is the only thing I have to rely on, but my recollections of the Houghton Club water when I was a lad are of a river running full and clear, filtered in the winter and spring months by irrigated meadows. These meadows also offered an 'early bite' for the farmers' livestock and a haven for duck, snipe and numerous other birds in the coldest months of the year. In summer and early autumn those same meadows supported an abundance of wild flowers, butterflies and frogs. In those days, too, there were one or two grinding water mills still in operation up and down the valley.

That was more than fifty years ago. It's a different story today and there seems little doubt to me that the present generation has messed things up good and proper with their modern farming practices, including the widespread use of herbicides and pesticides, fertilisers, silage, slurry and spray irrigation. There has been an explosion of fish farms up and down the valley with the constant danger of effluent from overcrowded stewponds and the wildfire spread of fish diseases. Industrial effluent, whether it is in the water or air-borne, or through spillage, is a continuing worry. The water authorities, too, have played their part in threatening the future of the Test through abstraction both from the rivers and from the aquifers.

Over the years the Test, like so many of our chalkstreams and rivers, has been abused by the farming and industrial community. Unless it is shown more care and consideration it could become little more than a drainage ditch unable to support any form of wildlife.

Take, for example, the considerable reduction in the number of salmon in the Middle Test. The decline of the salmon in all of our British rivers is sad and worrying. The number of fish falling to rod and line is decreasing annually. Years ago the spawning redds were a hive of activity; today there are few spawning fish and thus less chance of new generations in our rivers. We used to be able to count on three good runs of salmon as well as grilse, in the spring and summer. Now the only runs we can count on are of grilse, which come into our river in July and August; I feel that's because the grilse tend not to gather in the Faroes or the other well-known feeding grounds, but a few miles off the British coast where the high seas netsmen have not as yet found them.

Pity the poor salmon; from the moment it emerges from its egg sac as a fry it is in constant danger. In my view the biggest threat to the salmon comes from high seas netting. Today's sea-going salmon fishermen use highly sophisticated nylon filament nets – with a mesh that is small enough to trap even the immature fish – which are cast around huge shoals of fish either on their feeding grounds or in their passage up and down our coastline.

Those salmon that do escape the high seas netsmen are then intercepted and eaten by seals as the fish make for the rivers and their long swim upstream to the spawning redds. I have often watched seals in the Kinresort sea loch in the Outer Hebrides helping themselves as a run of fish came in on the tide, with a goodly number of black-backed gulls circling overhead waiting to mop up after the seals had taken their toll of the fish.

Poachers, too, are an age-old and constant menace as they cast their nets at the dead of night in the estuaries to capture fish which come in on the tide to start their return journey to the rivers to spawn.

Once a salmon gets into the river system it is vulnerable to the many diseases that lurk in its depths. UDN is a cold water disease, which means that the spring fish which come into the river some months before spawning are likely to be exposed to it twice: first when they run up river and again in the cold water months before they spawn in January. These seem to be the fish which suffer the most. The salmon that come into the river in the summer – when the water temperature is 50°F or more – are only exposed to UDN when the water temperature drops in the months before spawning and they seem to escape unscathed. Fortunately UDN is running out of steam on this river and 20 years after it first arrived I found only two fish that were affected by it; I hope we have seen the last of it.

Add the natural wastage of salmon which die after spawning to the dangers of netting, seals, poaching and disease, and it's no wonder the king of fish is rapidly declining, although the fish that die after spawning have hopefully accomplished what they came into our rivers to do.

Many people blame the river as it is today for the decline of the salmon, with the water more turbid and many of the spawning redds too heavily silted to allow life-giving oxygen to pass over the eggs. Others suggest that there are too many trout in the river, which feed on salmon parr. I'm not a great believer in these theories. What is true is that in low water years, when the outflow from the table trout farms up and down the valley is stronger than the current in the river, quite a few salmon get confused, swim up the outflow and get trapped behind the stewpond grids. The downstream migrating smolts in April also come up against a similar problem when they follow the stronger current of water as it is funnelled into the top end of the trout farm stewponds. Over the years I have released a number of smolts which have become trapped in this way at our stewponds in Stockbridge.

As a salmon fisher I have had endless conversations about the decline of the salmon. I often suggest that maybe we as anglers are not doing our bit to help the salmon. Why don't we introduce a daily limit, as on the Canadian rivers where anglers are allowed to take two fish a day but must then return all the others they catch?

Fortunately, there are moves afoot on many Scottish rivers to ban the use of bait for catching salmon: on the lower beats of the Tay in the autumn of 1989 it was reported that 200 fish were being taken every week by anglers using prawn or shrimp as bait.

Somehow I feel we have to give old Salar a helping hand. In some parts of the country, including the Test, the water authorities, fishery and estate owners and several associations have started to stock the rivers with smolts. I would favour supplementing this stocking with a widespread planting of well-grown, three-month-old fry. I say this because since father's days we have boosted the native brown trout population on our water with three-month-old trout fry every year and the result have been most encouraging in that the river now supports a good head of native fish. I therefore feel that the combination of stocking with farm-reared smolts and three-month-old fry gives us a double chance of founding a new dynasty of native Test salmon. Whichever policy is adopted, I hope that the wholesale restocking of our rivers, the banning of high seas netting and bait fishing, and a more sympathetic approach by rod and line anglers will one day restore the runs of these magnificent fish to their former glory.

It's not just the salmon that has suffered. At the other extreme my thoughts go to the common frog, which has almost totally disappeared from our 15 miles of the Middle Test.

In the spring, when I was a lad, the ditch running down to the river past

Riverside Cottage was full of frog spawn; come mid-July there were so many small frogs about that my father had to put a sack down across the scullery door to stop them invading the house. Today there are no frogs in that ditch and I have scarcely seen more than a handful up and down the river in the past several years. As far as I can tell the common frog was one of the first casualties of the use of such pesticides as DDT, dieldrin and aldrin, which were banned too late to save them and a number of other creatures; although some species have started to reappear on the river thanks to nature's resilience.

Ingenious though Man has been in inventing new chemicals to prevent bugs and blights destroying his crops, I sometimes feel that we are in too much of a hurry to treat the land with herbicides and pesticides before we understand their full effects. One simple example of this was the pesticide a farmer sprayed from the air to control a bug that was attacking oil-seed rape. Five colonies of bees were wiped out in one operation, because spraying was done at a time when the bees were gathering pollen and nectar from the rape fields. Now, before the farmers spray their fields, they contact local beekeepers so that the bees can be kept in their hives until the pesticide has lost its toxicity.

In the early 1900s there was quite a to-do about the metalling of the roads in and around Stockbridge and Houghton, with members of the Club fearing that the tarmacadam would somehow affect the purity of the river. They didn't realise that the tar wasn't the real danger, it was the smoothness of the surface it provided, which in a heavy rainstorm was washed clean of its deposits of oil, petrol, rubber and mud, the whole mess running off the road into the surrounding fields and into the watercourse.

Man has a lot to answer for. One change – for personal profit, with no regard for the side-effects of his actions – is the abandonment of the water-meadows. In grandfather's day these meadows provided farmers with a lush, early crop of spring grass which they fed to their livestock after the cattle and sheep had over-wintered on hay. But that wasn't its only purpose.

Throughout its course the River Test has both high and low river levels. At meadow-flooding time in January the water in the high level was purposely let out through organised hatchways and channels over the land on its way into the low level stream; a drainage system designed to get water trickling over all the land the farmers wanted to irrigate. This highly-skilled operation was carried out by drowners, men who with their calculating eye and drowning spades – narrow peat-cutting spades with long, sharp blades – knew exactly how and where to site their wooden hatchways to dam the river and cut drainage ditches that carried the water to left and right so that it drowned the whole field and not just the middle of it.

Today we can only imagine what it must have been like to see the whole river being passed over the land in stages, filtering out all the sediment before the water found its way back into the river. The end results were manifold: the river was gin-clear throughout the year; the water meadows enjoyed the benefit of mineral-rich silt and sediment; the removal of sediment from the river-bed encouraged the healthy growth of all the river-bed weeds, which in their turn also filtered out the remaining sediment in the river; and the farmer got his reward of fresh spring pastures.

By today's standards the work of the drowner would be too labour-intensive: money spent in this way to produce early spring grass would not be profitable. But the loss of these meadows has meant that the weed in the river is now the only filter, and it isn't able to cope with the immense amount of solids in suspension that the river now carries. Nowadays, when the springs break after the winter rains, the sheer volume of water contained within the river's banks scours out the river-bed, stirring up all the sediment and 'colouring' the water.

This colour in the river is added to by the riverkeepers up and down the Test Valley who in winter are busy clearing the mud and silt which has built up on the slow corners of their water; sediment which is passed on from one fishery to the next, never completely leaving the river.

This discolouration is not only unsightly, it also has a detrimental effect on the river weeds which grow early in the season because the colour shuts out the light. As a result, weed growth doesn't really get under way until midsummer when the flow of water subsides and the later growing weeds begin their growth. So, for several vital months the weeds which previously filtered the sediment out of the river are unable to do their job. The boffins tell us that nitrate levels in our river are 'acceptable' and the water quality is 'up to their standards', but are these standards high enough to ensure that in the years to come the Test doesn't become a coloured, lifeless river?

Although change has been a gradual process there is little doubt that the unsavoury weeds, such as starwort and blanket weed, have increased. During the long hot summer of 1989, blanket weed spread its tentacles all over the river and suffocated the good weeds. The following winter whole stretches of the river-bed, which had previously supported strong, healthy weed growth, were barren. I have never seen it so bad and I shall be interested to watch the outcome. I can only imagine that after such a summer the Houghton Club water will start the season with less weed, as will probably be the case with other stretches from the middle of the river downstream. The upper reaches are more fortunate in that their water is

Grandfather digging over the spawning shallows at Sheepbridge to free
them of silt

shallower and therefore has a sharper flow of water and cooler temperatures,
which has reduced the amount of blanket weed.

The water-meadows were also a tremendous asset in the winter months
to man and beast, because in cold winters when most of the still waters were
frozen over, the water-meadows were the only open, running waters in the
valley, so they offered all kinds of birds an attractive place to feed. Here in
the Middle Test in January the meadows were full of birds including pretty
well all of the duck family – including mallard, widgeon and teal. In cold
weather, geese and a multitude of snipe, plover and wagtails flighted in to
the water-meadows: each of them probing and sifting out the insects and
vegetation which were there in abundance.

It was also a great time for the shooters who would build their hides in the
meadows and wait for the birds to flight in.

Another threat to the river comes from the sheer number of people in the
area. From the 1800s to the early 1940s the Test Valley was made up of
small towns and villages, so human effluent was less of a problem than it

116

is today. In those days most of the village people had outdoor bucket lavatories, the so-called 'one holers'. The lucky ones living by the river had their one holers built over the water, or piped their sewage into it. Some with one holers who lived across the road from the river would, at dead of night, empty their buckets into the Test. But most played fair and buried the contents of their buckets in the garden.

Given the smallness of each village community it never seemed to affect the river's clarity and purity. It did no perceivable harm to its denizens. It was the way of the world then; septic tanks and main drains were to follow many years later.

Today, it's a different story as the country's population spreads across the landscape with new cities springing up where small market towns once existed. Take a town like Andover just north of Stockbridge on the River Anton, which is one of the River Test's main tributaries. It used to be a small market town. Now it is becoming a city, with new estates being built every year to house more and more people, all of whom need a tap to turn on for their drinking water and bath, a cistern to flush the lavatory and water for their washing machines.

The water to satisfy these needs has to come from somewhere, and – unlike London, which gets its water from man-made reservoirs – most of the homes in this valley get their mains water from the aquifers. Fifty years ago these stores of fresh, clean water supplied village wells and ensured the steady flow of the River Test.

Over the years, bore holes have been sunk into the aquifers to abstract more and more water for domestic needs. Today the village of Houghton takes its mains water from a bore hole adjacent to the Wallop Brook, which flows into the Test below Bossington Mill. Years ago, that brook had a good, strong flow all year round, except during drought years. Now every year the flow is less strong with a fair percentage of the volume of water in the brook 'topped up', so to speak, by the treated sewage effluent from Middle Wallop army base. The Wallop Brook has dried up only twice in my lifetime: during the 1976 and 1989 drought years. If those drought years were to be followed by mild dry winters with little or no water finding its way into the aquifer, the combination of a reduced flow of spring water and continued abstraction might have eventually turned the Wallop Brook into a drainage ditch.

My fear for the future is that if we continue to tap the aquifers to provide more and more homes with water, the River Test might one day exist only as a recycled water-drainage channel for the cities, towns and villages of the Test Valley.

As the human population increases in this valley, so their need for more loos, washing machines and dishwashers creates more effluent. In the days of the one holer the worst you ever got in the river was human effluent and some paper, which quickly disappeared. Today people use all sorts of bleaches, detergents and bug destroyers which, however well they are treated, always leave traces of their chemical base, which get into the river.

I don't have an instant solution to the problem: but someone, somewhere has to find an answer even if it does mean building unsightly reservoirs up and down the valley. We simply cannot continue to take fresh spring water out and replace it with man-made, treated water.

Anybody who lives in the countryside is aware of how farming methods have changed in the past fifty years, and while the record output from arable land has been remarkable – with four or more tons of cereals to the acre being produced – the way it has been achieved has damaged our environment. In my view, the Dig for Victory years of the Second World War, when farmers were encouraged to turn over more of their land for food production, was the beginning of the end for traditional, environmentally friendly farming methods.

It may have been necessary at the time, but the landscape has never fully recovered from the destruction of hedgerows to provide extra productive acreage – or from the ploughing up of our uplands of gorse and grass for crop production. Now the uplands are fields of barley and some of the valley floor – once meadows full of reasonable grazing and wild flowers – has been turned over to maize.

In the last thirty years as more land came under the plough, new herbicides and pesticides were discovered to control weeds and to get rid of insects which fed on the crops. The land produced more for us to eat at a price.

Years ago, the valley floor on either side of the River Test was a haven for butterflies and wild flowers. Today tortoise-shell, orange tip, little blues and browns, peacock, and red admiral butterflies are not so numerous – although they are still to be seen – and the rich carpet of kingcup, ragged robbin, marsh orchid, yellow-rattle and cowslips has all but disappeared. Now most of the wild flowers that remain cling to the river's edge, their only sanctuary from herbicides.

Fortunately there are still tracts of land untouched by herbicides and pesticides: Stockbridge Common Down and Marsh and the acres around Farley Mount have escaped the chemical sprays and as a result are alive with butterflies, grasshoppers and wild flowers. I hope these wild places will be increased as a result of the Government subsidy offered to landowners willing to set aside some of their land to lie fallow and wild.

There is also a move towards organic farming in many parts of the country, which may well be a good thing in the long run, though I'm not so sure that total conversion to these early farming methods will produce all the food we need to keep the country going.

The greatest danger to any environment is overcrowding, whether it's chicken, pigs, sheep, fish or human beings. Put too many of them together and you're asking for trouble. Such trouble faces us in the Test Valley because the recent expansion of fish farms means the river has to support more fish now than ever before. Trout farms which raise more and more table fish in as little space as possible increase the chance of disease among their own fish, and such disease quickly finds its way into the river, affecting everyone up and downstream.

The ideal fish farm should have a plentiful water supply, with the number of fish restricted – according to the size of the stewpond – and there should be an adequate gradient between the inflow and outflow so that the stewponds can be drained down easily and cleaned out thoroughly.

I try to keep my stewponds that way and would never attempt to raise more fish in them than can be sustained by the amount of water available to me. But with the arrival of the trout farms, one by one diseases I had previously only read about in American fish farming journals have appeared in our river system: whirling disease, then PKD, ERM and IPN, followed by a medical dictionary full of weird and wonderful names, each of them potential killers. In my father's day and in my early years as Head Keeper of the Houghton Club waters, furunculosis and saprolignia were the only two diseases that gave us any worries, and we knew exactly how to deal with them.

I have great sympathy for table trout farmers, I know they are under considerable pressure to produce quantity. But their stewponds are like giant digestive systems, taking in as much water as they can at one end, running it through densely populated channels where the trout are fed high-protein pellets, with the result that the water which passes out of the stewponds and back into the main river is heavily polluted with effluent, whether it's trout faeces or a colourful tinge of Malachite Green.

So what is to be done? I would prevent the building of any more fish farms in the Test Valley; maybe there should be some form of legislation to force fish farmers to build settling ponds or lagoons and insist that they should, like anyone who creates industrial waste, dispose of it in such a way that it does not harm the environment. Maybe this effluent would make a good fertiliser; after all, it's full of protein, nitrates and all sorts of other goodies which must have a secondary and beneficial use to someone.

What is not in doubt is that these fish farmers owe it to the river to clean up their act. As a youngster I had it drummed into me that all of us who live on the Test and are associated with it were the keepers of a valuable inheritance. We were its guardians and when the time came for us to hand that inheritance on to our children, grandchildren and great grandchildren, it should be in the same or better condition.

In my grandfather's days and certainly when father was Head Keeper, otters were trapped by all the keepers on the river. Otters are nocturnal creatures with a penchant for eels. They were also responsible for killing quite a few trout, getting into the stewponds containing our one-year-old fish and in one night killing anything up to fifty fish, leaving perhaps forty partially-eaten trout on the bank. To them it was a game; to grandfather and father it was a serious loss of fish.

An otter trap is a deadly machine with large, double jaws and a hefty spring. As the otters hunted by night these traps had to be set on the bank where the otters were known to come out of the water during a night's fishing. Under my father's guidance I learned how to tell the difference between where otters entered the water – these were areas on the bank where the grass was flattened and pushed forward towards the water – which was not a place to set your trap because the otter would simply slide over it. What you had to look for was a similar disturbance of the bankside vegetation where the grass was flattened away from the river by the otters as they pulled themselves out of the water and on to the bank: that's where you set your trap.

In many ways I am very sad that the otter has disappeared from our water: I never like to see the last of any species. They were lovely, playful animals and I count it as something of a privilege that I can remember seeing them come to the surface on a warm July evening, snort loudly and dive back down in search of food; I will never forget the evening I saw a family of otters playing on the bank below North Head.

Incidentally, when the film *Tarka the Otter* was being made I supplied the 'props' – the fish and eels fed to the animal star of the film. The River Tamar setting of the film was simulated in an area of park land a few miles from Stockbridge.

In practical, riverkeeping terms, the disappearance of the otter from our water means we have one less predator to watch out for, and there are more than enough of those, particularly among the valley's bird life. The birds see the river as a moving conveyor belt of food, whether it's the growing trout, their eggs, or the lush growth of vegetation both in the river and along its banks.

So far, touch wood, mink have not presented a problem on the Test. Over the last thirty years the occasional mink has been caught and we once had a scare when some disgruntled neighbours of a mink farm near Andover released the inmates because no one was prepared to take action over the stench that wafted into their homes. Fortunately the mink were soon recaptured. I continue to stay alert to the danger of mink and remember a time in the Avon Valley when quite a few were trapped in one year. If mink descended on us in any great strength we would have a real problem.

In grandfather's day the dabchick was always reckoned to be one of the riverkeeper's enemies and according to the record books he killed close on 150 a year. Most authorities will tell you that the dabchick lives happily on a diet of minnows, shrimp, dragonfly nymphs, water beetles and other aquatic insects and molluscs. Having lived on this river sixty-odd years I can authoritatively add small trout and trout ova to that list, having observed a pair of dabchicks scratching around in the shallows until they cleared a trout redd of a good many of its eggs. I shoot a few most years, but I usually leave these playful little birds alone, although my fishermen have been known to curse them for diving into the water so neatly that they could be mistaken for a rising fish.

Kingfishers are grand birds and to get a glimpse of one during a day's angling is a great bonus. Although they will eat small trout as part of their diet, they seem to prefer minnows and are not regarded as a pest by riverkeepers. Anyway, life is hard enough for these beautiful streaks of orange and sapphire lightning: they suffer badly, as do other birds, in very cold winters when the constant freezing temperatures drive the minnows into deeper water and the ponds and river margins ice up, cutting off the kingfishers' food supply. Many died on this river during the Arctic winter of 1962–3.

Unlike the dabchick and the kingfisher, the heron is one of the river-keeper's traditional enemies, adept as it has become in taking young fish from the stewponds, finding a way through even the most clever netting system. At spawning time we have to keep an eye out for the heron that wades into the shallows and spears a large spawning fish just for the fun of it, knowing it has no chance of eating it. But the heron is a protected bird today so all we can do is scare them off the water.

Fifteen years ago if a cormorant was seen on our waters it was recorded in the book as an uncommon sighting. Nowadays I have seen as many as twenty in one day, every one of them an expert fisher. It's not as if they only visit for one day and return to their coastal homes at night. They have recently taken to staying overnight, setting up their temporary homes in the tall poplars and any dead trees down the bank. Frankly, I would rather have fifty heron than one cormorant. They are birds that may look cumbersome in flight, but in the water they swim like seals.

As far as I can tell, there are two reasons for the increase in the number of cormorants on our water through the late autumn and winter: storms at sea, which churn up the sea bed and make it impossible for the cormorant to spot fish may be one reason; another may be the heavy stocking policy of most of the fisheries on the Test, which means there are plenty of fish all over the river for the birds to feed on. I also think the recent explosion in the number of fish farms and the inevitable escapees into the river has contributed to the Test's popularity as a feeding ground for the cormorant.

Along with the cormorant the swan is another major nuisance. I keep reading and hearing that the swan population is on the decrease. That may be true of somewhere like the Sahara Desert, but here on the Middle Test and on the Avon there seem to be more every year.

Two or three swans are not much of a problem, but when you get, as we do, a herd of up to one hundred at a time ripping up the weed, they are a real menace, endangering the river's ability to support its plant, insect and fish life.

The swan is one of nature's vegetarians and ranunculus is one of its favourite plants. It doesn't take a great deal of imagination to realise that in a week one hundred swans can reduce a luscious growth of ranunculus, and all the shrimps and insects clinging to the weed, into a bare stretch of river-bed. If they are on your river through the year, the river-bed, in a very short time, will be bereft of weed and insect life. Any trout that were lying behind the protective cover of that weed and feeding off the insects washed out from it will soon move on, up or downstream, in search of another home. So within weeks, a productive stretch of river you had been maintaining over the years has become totally useless.

Many years ago, riverkeepers in our area received a special dispensation from the courts which allowed them to cull the swan population on their waters to a manageable level. That's not the case today, unfortunately, so the best we can do is chase them away.

Another bird that seems irrevocably to be on the increase is the Canada goose: in 1953 there were 3000 in the UK, in 1988 that population had grown more than tenfold to 40,000. In this valley I put the increase down to the people who originally kept them as garden pets. They bred freely on the ornamental ponds and soon their progeny took flight and through the years have multiplied, adapting well to their surroundings. We were all very excited some years ago at seeing our first pair of Canada geese in the valley.

Now I despair when I see them arrive on our water in flights of 50 or more.

Outside of the breeding season, the Canada goose is a very gregarious bird, which means you can get as many as 80 or more all together at one time. It's not that they are any danger to the river, because their main diet is grass and corn. For the arable farmer the Canada goose is a real threat when it takes to eating his young cereal crops. To riverkeepers and anglers alike, they are a nuisance, making a terrible mess on the bank, which is unpleasant and unsightly. They can also, through sheer weight of numbers, cover the available water on a Beat, thus making it impossible for fish to rise and fishermen to cast to them.

Riverkeepers are professionals, experts in the ways of the river and its wildlife. For them to do their jobs properly – which includes nurturing, maintaining and protecting their rivers from pollution and disease – they should be given new powers to control the wildlife population on their waters: not as with the otter to destroy a species, but to control the population of each species so that they can create a healthy balance between those waterborne creatures in their charge and the visitors who are poised, through over-population, to upset it.

IX

A DAY'S PLAY

THE Houghton Club is founded on tradition, a tradition which stretches back more than 150 years to a time when roads were dirt tracks cut through the rolling downlands of the Test Valley, when people travelled to Stockbridge by mail coach and post-chaise, and the pace of life was slower.

From the foundation of the Houghton Club in 1822 to the present day, members have always gathered in the clubroom on the first floor of the Grosvenor Hotel in Stockbridge – a tradition guaranteed in 1918 when the Club bought the hotel at auction.

Another custom that has survived for well over a century and a half has been the 'keeper's favourites': those members who fished regularly with my grandfather, my father and myself.

My grandfather's favourite was Arthur Gilbey, the member who introduced the whipping rod to the Houghton Club in the 1890s. Gilbey was what Waller Hills described as a member of the 'modern school' of Club member, one of the first to bring new dressings of flies, 000 hooks (which are equivalent to today's number 7), and finer gut.

Along with Gilbey came considerable changes to the traditions. No longer did members only come down for the grannom hatches of April and the mayfly of May and June. A blue winged olive season was introduced and members fished through the long, hot days of June and July, and again through September to the season's end.

My father's favourite was Sir Harold Gillies – the man who pioneered modern plastic surgery. He was always thought to be a bit of an eccentric, but when it came to flyfishing he was a great experimenter, which caught father's fancy a bit.

My own particular favourite was Sir Laurence Dunne, the Chief Metropolitan Magistrate. He was a fine fisherman, an inquisitive entomologist and botanist – in every way a great angler and countryman – and an amusing and articulate raconteur. Together we made a fine team. We were a winning combination of horse and jockey, whether we were fishing the Houghton Club waters or enjoying winter days and evenings in his drawing room at Ham Mill, on the Kennet in Berkshire, either tying flies or discussing the way of a trout with a fly.

Many's the time I stood outside Sir Laurence's mill and watched as he fed the trout he kept in the pond below the mill stream. Among them was a particularly deep-bellied brown trout of around 7 lb, which was Sir Laurence's favourite. It was a fish he had caught perhaps a dozen times and he fed it regularly as one would feed a pet. He was so attached to it that it formed the centrepiece of one of his many amusing stories:

Before he sat on the Bench at Bow Street Sir Laurence was a circuit judge, and on one 'tour' he phoned home to ask that some important papers should be sent down to him. Grey, his butler, answered the phone and after Sir Laurence had given instructions regarding the documents he enquired, 'How's the old trout, Grey?'

'Her ladyship is well, thank you sir,' came the reply.

I learned a lot from the time I spent with Sir Laurence, and I hope, through the years, he learned something from me; together we enjoyed over twenty-five years of angling, writing, conversation and companionship.

What always made me feel good was when he told other Club members that with Mick's service you would 'double your bag'. That wasn't necessarily true, but coming from a person of such natural and consummate talent with rod and fly, it was quite a compliment.

I recognised that my greatest asset came from my grandfather and father: my keen eyesight. The experiences I had as a result of this quality gave me unequalled knowledge of my river and its bed and of the fly that hatched month-on-month at specific times of the day and evening.

As a keeper, one goes to the river, on whatever Beat, with what I call a 'prepared fish' or two. These are the result of the mental notes made about good trout which have been spotted in certain lies over the days of working on the river. In fact, I never walk home to lunch without putting on my Polaroid glasses and making accurate mental notes of the fish I have seen. In my view, such daily exercise is a must for keepers who take rods to the river. What has never ceased to amaze me is how much information one person can store in his mind.

This ability, which I have come across in most other keepers, enabled me

Sir Laurence Dunne waiting for the rise below the cattle bridge at
Longstock Mill

to take Sir Laurence to a spot where I knew a fish was lying, suggest a fly
pattern that would tempt the trout to rise, and know that he would follow
my suggestion with such a careful and accurate cast that the trout would do
just that. He was a joy to fish with.

However, the only way to appreciate the bond which has always existed
between the Houghton Club's members and guests and my grandfather,
father and myself, is to take you back to the early Sixties and 'a day's play'
with Sir Laurence.

As I have already said, the Houghton Club is founded on tradition, with
rituals which date back to 1822 when its twelve original members devised
the Club's rules. Central to this tradition is the clubroom, a fine old room on
the first floor of the Grosvenor Hotel overlooking Stockbridge High Street.
Here the walls are hung with portraits of members past and present,
landscapes of our beloved River Test, caricatures, photographs and stuffed

and mounted fish. The clubroom also holds a library of old and new fishing books and the Club's record books: stout, hand-crafted, leather-bound volumes which have stood as a permanent record of every member's days on the water, every fish caught and every fly used since 1822.

The atmosphere of the clubroom is leisurely and relaxed. It is an inner sanctum where some of the most influential and powerful men in the land have exchanged views on affairs of state. But the most important conversations here have been the swapped yarns, large and small, about the members' skill and delicacy with those collections of fur, feather and silk which have so fascinated flyfishers over the past two hundred years or so.

By gentlemen's club standards the room is not particularly grand and is without the usual oak-panelling. It has the look of a comfortable dining room in a modest manor house. Gathered around the open fireplace are deep leather armchairs and a sofa. But the real focal point of the room is the long, polished oak dining table by the window. It is here that every member, without exception, gathers in the morning to discuss his day and choose a Beat on the river, and returns again for supper before the evening rise.

For the last twenty-eight years during the flyfishing season, I have walked, as my father did, up the broad staircase to the clubroom after breakfast, knocked and waited for permission to enter. On that day, twenty-five years ago, the scene was much as it has always been.

In one corner a member was finishing off *The Times* crossword, another fiddled with a box of flies, looked up casually and asked whether a small Rough Olive was a good opening fly for the morning sport. In one of the armchairs another member was idly flicking through the *Financial Times*, grunting as he ran a practised eye over the day's play in the Stock Exchange.

But dominating the room, one arm leaning casually on the mantelshelf over the fireplace, was the powerful figure of Sir Laurence Dunne. He had a military bearing, a handsome head of greying dark hair and a slim salt and pepper moustache. His manner was such that he could either turn you to stone or invite you to join him in a drink.

'Morning Mick,' he said, eyeing me with the steady, penetrating gaze of a man used to handing down justice from the bench of the Metropolitan Magistrates' Court in Bow Street. 'How's the weather looking?'

'It's set fair, Sir Laurence, and what wind there is is light from the north. There's a fair amount of sunshine forecast, so we should have a fine day's fishing.'

'Now,' he said, immediately gaining the undivided attention of the gentlemen in the room, who recognised him to be one of the two most senior members present, 'the morning's beats. Maggie, you're the most recent arrival. Where would you like to fish this morning?'

'Maggie' was Sir Ivan Magill, the pioneering anaesthetist, and, looking to me for advice, he suggested the Borough Marsh Beat, which runs downstream from the High Street bridge in sight of the church. I nodded my approval. I knew no one had fished there for some days. It's not a popular Beat with members because its rather swampy going, but it was a favourite of Sir Ivan's as he once caught twenty-one trout from it in mayfly. On that day, a Lance Corporal on leave and out for a stroll with his dog watched as Sir Ivan struggled with so many fish. The soldier offered to carry his catch back to the Grosvenor Hotel and received a brace for his trouble.

'Ben, where would you like to fish?' asked Sir Laurence, casting his gaze to the member reading the *Financial Times*. 'If your shares are up, I'd suggest Machine; if they're down, try Upper Park.'

'All's well with my world,' replied Mr Bengough, folding the paper in his lap. 'I'll take Machine. There was a damn fine fish under the poplars when I was last down. . . .'

'It's still there, sir,' I said, 'but you'll have to be careful not to show yourself as you creep past. And I'd start with a large fly like a Caperer.' I knew this was a brilliant suggestion; he hardly used any other fly.

Remember, this was the early Sixties. Ten years before, in the first two weeks of June, I would have been safe in recommending a Spent Gnat for the late afternoon and early evening when the female mayfly returns to the water to oviposit. But in the late Fifties, strong north-easterly winds prevented the females from returning to the water. The mayfly didn't return to the Houghton Club waters until 1978 when we had a massive upstream migration. This migration of large, gossamer-winged adult mayflies is truly a wonder of nature. I have been lucky enough to witness it twice; it's a sight you never forget.

Sir Laurence continued to sort out the members' Beats for the morning. 'Now, Murray, where would you like to fish,' he asked, taking a small, well-worn aluminium fly box from his coat pocket and casting a satisfied glance over its contents.

'I favour Bossington,' replied Mr T. Murray Sowerby – one of the Houghton Club's great benefactors and a man as deadly with the fly as Sir Laurence.

'Good. . . . Then I'll take Upper Park Stream,' said Sir Laurence, putting his fly box away and turning, to me. 'You'll be with me today, Mick, is that right?'

'Yes, Sir Laurence,' I replied, 'that will be a pleasure.'

The Houghton Club water is 15 miles in length, divided into fourteen Beats, so even on a busy day with say, fifteen members and their guests down, the Beats are easily divisible and no one feels he has to crowd another's water.

The beauty of our stretch of the River Test is that although I may have a favourite Beat or two, I am quite happy to go where I am sent; all the Beats yield fish. Sometimes the rise is better on one Beat than another, but they are all well stocked. The weather, however, has to be taken into account because some Beats are more sheltered than others and on a breezy day this can make all the difference.

One thing is for certain, though, whatever Beat a fisherman chooses, he will always feel he should have picked another one.

'We can take the car to the bottom of the Beat at Park Bridge,' said Sir Laurence.

Park Bridge is the natural border that separates Upper and Lower Park Streams. These are both fairly well sheltered stretches of water and very good for spotting fish.

While Sir Laurence surveyed the water I put up his rod, a 9ft split cane wand, which was perfect for covering all the water. Today, I suppose, he'd use a carbon or boron rod.

Sir Laurence was a great one for caring for his flyfishing equipment, varnishing his rods every winter and repairing old whippings. The line he used was an AirCel AFTM6 floating line, with a long nylon cast of around 10ft tapering down to a 4 lb point. He always favoured fishing with a white fly line, which I feel is a distinct advantage, especially in poor light.

Before handing the rod over to Sir Laurence, I lightly greased the last yard of the fly line to prevent it sinking, which can have a detrimental effect on the strike. For some reason even the most expensive floating fly line tends to sink where the nylon cast is joined to it. Maybe it's the added weight of the needle knot joining cast to line. I don't know.

'What fly, Mick, that's the question of the morning,' said Sir Laurence, casting a practised eye over the water for signs of any hatching fly.

'I thought I'd tie on a hackled Caperer,' I replied. 'It's a good fly, what I'd call a "surprise fly", and a good opener for the fish which shows once or is seen in the water.'

'Well,' said Sir Laurence, taking his rod from me, 'with luck we'll see some olives hatching around the middle of the day, and if the wind drops this evening, we'll get a hatch of pale wateries and see a few sedges. I suppose the iron blue has pretty well disappeared. It was another disappointing mayfly, Mick.'

129

'Yes, it was, sir. And those that did hatch were mostly eaten by the birds,' I replied. 'I sometimes think members should take a shotgun to pop off the sparrows and chaffinches, then there would be a few mayfly left to reproduce. But I believe there was a good hatch again down at Mottisfont. Probably because it's a lot more sheltered down there. In fact, Sir Laurence, I wouldn't wonder if those wooded areas below us aren't going to be the saviour of the mayfly on our waters.'

'So where do you recommend we start, Mick?' he asked.

'I've checked below the shallows and I've had a look under the bridge for the odd tail or two, but there are only a couple of small wild brownies in the usual lie, so we might as well move on upstream. The current on this lower stretch of the Beat is fairly even, but the weed has grown since the late April weed cut. This means that the lumps of carrot weed will create channels of water running at different speeds, so we'll have to be careful not to get any drag on the fly.'

We had started the day on the right bank, so in an hour or so we would get the best of the light for spotting fish.

'There,' I said, pointing to a good-size rise under the bank on our side of the stream. 'There, just in front of that overhanging flag.'

We walked up, slowly and carefully, to within casting distance of the movement.

'Let's see if it comes again,' I said.

The importance of making a mark cannot be stressed enough and it's not easy when a fish is away from the bank on a wide stretch of the river. But there is always something – a piece of weed, a patch of gravel, a plant on the bank, even a cow's backside as long as it's not moving too quickly – you can use as a marker.

Too many fishers race forward to cast when a 'oncer' shows. This is always a mistake because if you don't mark where the fish is lying in the water first then the scale or distance between the flyfisher and the trout changes, making an accurate first-time cast very difficult. Anyway, a hurried movement will often put the fish down as it gets a glimpse of the angler.

'He's shown again,' said Sir Laurence.

'Are you sure it wasn't a dabchick?' I replied.

'Oh no, I saw the beginning of the move to the fly. I know it was a fish, but I'll give him another minute, maybe he'll come again,' said Sir Laurence. 'We can see quite a bit of water from here and anyway, when the sun comes from behind that cloud you can creep forward and get a better look at him.'

'Baffled!' by Sir Edwin Landseer

'A Member of the Club'
by J. M.W. Turner

'The Boot Inn in the village of Houghton'
by Sir Francis Chantrey

'Sir Francis Chantrey "Blowing"'
by George Jones

'The Casting Net' by Frederick R. Lee

'Yes, he's there all right,' I said, 'virtually underneath that overhanging flag, so if you pop it up just outside the flag he should come to it.'

'He's truly a Corban fish . . . a gift from God.' Sir Laurence always said this if he felt a fish was a certain taker. He explained it was Greek for a God-given fish.

By now he had edged forward a yard or so and was lengthening his line in a series of false casts. There was a light downstream wind, which is ideal for throwing the 'shepherd's crook' cast. This is a casting technique which leaves the line and most of the cast outside the fish, while the fine point and the fly go over it. Such a cast is not difficult with practice and is often the only way you can put a fly accurately to a fish under your own bank, though it's well nigh impossible with a strong following wind or for a right-handed caster on the left bank. Ideally, though, it is better to be ambidextrous, something I learned and practised when I was much younger under my father's gentle and patient tuition.

Keeping his rod low, Sir Laurence made his cast with a good deal of drive, checking the throwing hand when the line was almost extended to make the cast swivel. The fly flicked left . . . the fish rose . . . got him.

Sir Laurence had always been a great exponent of the slow strike, but by God it was always a firm one, a real line zinger.

'He's not strong,' called Sir Laurence, 'but he's active and looks to be a decent fish to start the day.'

I picked up the net and stood downstream of Sir Laurence as he played the fish. There was no hurry to put the net in the water, because if Sir Laurence ran to form he would get the trout's head up and slide him on top of the water. All I had to do was slip the net under the fish and dip him out.

'A good start, Sir Laurence,' I said as I weighed the 2 lb 12oz brownie in the net.

Using a large fly, as we were that June morning, the strike can be a slow one: the fish rises to the fly, takes it and turns down, so the tempo is rise, pause, then strike. I always feel that the strike should go in step with the stream, so if you're fishing a fast flowing stretch your strike is a little quicker. If the river is slow and dreamy, the strike is slower, but there must always be that vital pause, otherwise you will take the fly away from the fish and a chance will be missed.

I removed the hook from the trout's jaw; it was embedded in the 'scissors' and would never have come loose. I then washed the fly, and dried off the excess water with amadou – a fungus with the texture of soft leather. Nowadays I favour a dry fly powder, which dries and reconditions the fly for immediate re-use. I then smeared the silicone grease I used for the end of

Sir Laurence's fly line onto the hackles of the fly with my thumb and forefinger.

'I don't know about you, Mick,' said Sir Laurence, 'but I don't think all these modern potions in bottles and canisters are the equal of that silicone fly line grease.'

'Agreed,' I said, 'to my mind those new-fangled floatants are very wasteful and often they don't work too well, either.'

We walked slowly upstream, stopping occasionally to search the water in a likely lie for the merest flicker of fin or mouth.

'There, look,' said Sir Laurence, pointing upstream to one side of a line of trees. 'They look like olive spinners to me, Mick.'

'Males, too,' I said, 'and they wouldn't be dancing up and down in the air like that if they weren't expecting a few females.'

'We'll have some fine sport with a Lunn's Particular later, when the females return to the water.'

'Absolutely, Sir Laurence.'

We walked on upstream, past the trees and through the cloud of spinners. We were approaching the lower end of Horseshoe Bend, which well describes the kink in the river ahead of us. The river ran quite deep as we approached the corner and scanned the water systematically from left to right for signs of a fish.

It's in this deeper water, close in to your own bank, that fish tend to lie, and they're easy to miss unless you're both very cautious and scan the water thoroughly.

There is also a swallow-hole in the bed of the river, which has been there for as long as I can remember. The swallow-hole takes water to the low level stream called Black Lake. The Test Valley has a whole system of high and low level arms of the river, which date back to the days when the mill owners and farmers created irrigation channels to take the flow off the main river. They also controlled the flow to flood the water-meadows, which ensured fresh, spring pasture for cattle and sheep.

Occasionally, you will find a fish cruising round the back eddy of this blowhole because a lot of food collects in the constant whirl of water.

Above us the river begins to shallow again quite quickly.

'Didn't your grandfather have something to do with these shallows, Mick?'

'Yes, sir. It must have been quite a job back in those days when the only transport was horse and cart and the only tools were shovels. Grandfather filled in this length of the water to create a spawning bed for the fish, so load after load of gravel was tipped in and then spread by hand to create shallows where trout could create their redds.'

The deep water below these shallows is perfect for fish to lie and feed. Besides the surface food, nymphs and shrimp in abundance are continually washing out, shaken from the weeds upstream to flow down into the deeper water.

'Stand still,' I said, resting an arm on Sir Laurence's sleeve as I saw two good brownies chasing one another. When trout behave like that it's usually because one has encroached on the other's territory. 'If we just wait here a moment,' I continued, 'those two will soon settle back into their respective lies and we can have a pop at them.

'One of them looks settled now, Sir Laurence, and, yes, it looks like he just took a nymph.'

'Should I try a Caperer, Mick?'

'Yes, that should be okay. But hang on, I'll give you a line. There, immediately below the trailing bullrush spike, about opposite that tussock.'

'I'll try a short cast and go a bit wide,' said Sir Laurence, as he pulled the nylon cast through the top ring of his rod and flicked out one false cast, then another, finishing with the accurate, feather-light landing of the Caperer a few feet short of the trout.

'Try it another 3ft longer and 3ft to the right.'

Sir Laurence pulled two more lengths of line from his reel and cast again.

'It's a little wide,' I warned him, 'but, yes, the fish is coming across, I can see the white under his chin. Leave the fly where it is, there. . . .

The fish rose, sipped slowly at the fly and turned down with it. Sir Laurence struck and the fish, feeling the hook, turned sharply upstream and made a dash for the weeds below the shallows. If we have a bit of luck playing this fish, I thought, we'll have another in the bag.

I needn't have worried, it was very rare that Sir Laurence ever lost a fish once he'd struck.

Removing the hook, I ran a finger down the cast for any unwanted knots. Our back cast did just flick a tall spear, so I checked for any signs of wear; something I do every so often in a day's fishing. Such occasional checks can mean the difference between landing and losing a strong, fighting Houghton Club trout. Many's the time the penny hasn't dropped until three fish are lost and then an inspection of the cast reveals a hook with a broken point.

Two fish in the bag now, the second a little heavier at 3lb. I've often been on these spotting sorties and it's not always as straightforward or as successful as this morning. That's because such a great deal depends on the accuracy of the fisherman's cast once I have explained the line it should take.

Of course, there is nothing like the first cast at a fish. The more casts you make, the more likely you are to spook it with a throw that's too long or too short, too much to the right or left, or too heavy. Everyone knows the feeling, and the result.

But with Sir Laurence, I had few fears about both his accuracy and lightness.

'In all your time at the water, Mick,' remarked Sir Laurence, as I removed the fly from the trout's jaw, 'how often is casting the main topic of conversation?'

'Sir Laurence,' I replied, recognising him to be a man who needed little in the way of tuition, 'it's so easy to be critical of your casting technique when you can actually see the fish lying in the water. But when you're fishing for a rising trout, the accuracy or inaccuracy is perhaps not so noticeable, because the fish is looking for food, and like the last fish you took, Sir Laurence, it's willing to move to take what looks like food.

'Telling someone they should cast 6in. more to the trout's left or right is rather splitting hairs. Fish have exceptional eyesight and see more than we think. But there do appear to be special spots where the fly falls which have special attractions, like just behind the fish and to the right or left of the middle of its back.

'The main thing is to let the fish see the fly as it lands, even if it is behind what you believe to be its angle of vision.'

Sir Laurence nodded, then looked sharply upstream to the second of the two fish in the shallows.

'That second brownie seems to have settled down, Sir Laurence. He's a cock fish,' I said, seeing the trout's unmistakably aggressive-looking, hooked lower jaw or kipe. 'He's plain enough to see, lying on that gravel bed above the patch of ranunculus.'

'Hang on, Mick, which fish do you mean? Him on that patch of silt?'

'No, Sir Laurence, not the one on the far side, that's a grayling, I mean the one in the middle where the shadow of that ash tree shows on the water. But be careful, there's quite a drag there. The run under our bank is much more pacy than that beyond the fish, and the weed in front of it is creating a bit of a boil, so the fly won't fish for long.'

I needn't have bothered explaining the ways of the water to Sir Laurence. He was an expert in such circumstances. As I talked he dropped to one knee and crept forward to a position a yard or so upstream of being opposite the fish.

He worked out line in a series of false casts, eventually casting some two or three yards more line than the distance between him and the fish. He checked the line with one hand and pulled it back to put slack in the forward end, and pointed the rod tip upstream to produce a curve as line and fly landed softly on the water.

Pointing his rod tip at the fly he followed its progress downstream to the fish, lifting off when the fly was well below his target.

For some reason the trout ignored the Caperer, expertly cast though it was.

'Maybe it was too big a fly,' he said.

'Shall we try a spinner, like a Houghton Ruby or a Lunn's Particular?' I suggested.

Sir Laurence looked up from his fly box and took a Particular out between his thumb and forefinger. 'Something like that?' he said, grinning broadly. I tied the fly onto his cast.

Using the same expert casting technique to allow for the inevitable drag caused by the mix of currents, the Particular landed a few feet from the trout. It rose, and compensating for the slack line on the water, Sir Laurence struck a split-second earlier to pick the line off the water, and a third fish was securely hooked and guided expertly to the waiting net.

'Size of fly, Mick,' said Sir Laurence, as I took the fly from the trout's jaw, 'how important is that?'

'Very,' I said, not looking up. 'Today's fishers tend to continue casting a large fly to a fish and in consequence put it down. Three to four chucks with a big fly, satisfying yourself that you've covered it successfully, is more than enough. If it refuses, go down a size or two.

'So many times I've joined rods on the bank and they've said, "There was a good fish rising here. I've tried several casts with a large fly and he hasn't risen again."

'All I can think is, "I'm not surprised. You've clouted that fly time and time again over its head and after it has had a good look and refused it, why assume the fish is going to change its mind suddenly and grab hold of it?"

'No . . . change perhaps to a larger pattern for a cast of two, then try a smaller fly, particularly to a rising trout. In my experience such a fish is more likely to be tempted by a smaller fly unless the cast is heavy, which will put the fish down. Often sheer persistence with a small fly will take fish. Persistence with a large fly will simply put a trout down.

'Remember, when there is a large hatch of fly on the water, the fish is spoiled for choice. So try a pattern totally unlike the fly he is taking, and be persistent, changing flies fairly often, and going down in size as you change. Eventually the trout will make a mistake.

'Needless to say, Sir Laurence,' I smiled, recognising that the mayfly was absent that year, 'during mayfly or, as we may get tonight, a decent evening of fishing when there are sedges about, the larger fly does work every time.'

Upstream of the shallows one or two smaller fish were moving, but the sun had moved round to its highest, midday point. 'Time for a wet,' said Sir Laurence, walking ahead of me to the Savill bench.

Six of these comfortable bankside benches – made from untreated oak by one of Sir Eric Savill's craftsmen in the Savill Gardens at Windsor – were presented by him to the Houghton Club and placed at various vantage points along the water.

Settling on our Savill bench, I unpacked the cider and sandwiches.

'Have I ever told you about G. M. La Branche, Mick? Now he was a regular American gentleman and the first man to show me the shepherd's crook cast. What an expert he was.

'I knew him well, you know, as did your father. I reckon his secret lay in a stiffish rod and a line with no perceptible taper, a flat 3x gut cast and a fairly bushy fly.

'As far as I could tell, the cast depended on a premature shoot of the line when his fly was about half way or more towards the trout. This meant that towards the end of the cast the line was pulling the fly along after it and landed well upstream of the trout, making a nice, large curve.

'Mind you, it required perfect timing to make a good cast every time, particularly if such a big fly was to land accurately and gently.'

Munching on my sandwich I thought for a moment. 'That sounds too good for me,' I said after a moment's thought. 'I'll stick to getting as close as possible and fishing as square as possible to avoid drag.'

There was a light northerly breeze blowing, the sun was passing through its highest point and we had three good Houghton Club trout in the bag. There was but a sparse hatch of fly.

'We should find some fish above us,' I remarked, packing the remains of lunch into my bag. 'When I walked up here a few days ago there was a good fish or two at the lower end of the top shallows. But with so little in the way of fly about, we'll have to continue spotting our fish. There's always the chance we'll come across a few "bulging": intercepting nymphs as the insects rise to the surface to become mature flies.'

I stepped forward and in so doing recognised my mistake. As I have always told my anglers, watch out for the fish under your own bank. I had just broken that cardinal rule and watched helplessly as a good-sized brownie made for the cover of the weeds a few yards upstream of us.

With any other fisher I'd say nothing, but with Sir Laurence I was able to openly admit my mistake.

'I'll make a mental note of the spot,' I reassured him, 'he may well be back once he has settled down, and we can have a go at him when we walk back to the car. If not, there's always another day for that one.'

I don't always tell the rod I'm fishing with if I scare a fish like that, mainly because we Lunns have a reputation to maintain. I'd rather hear a member say, 'Mick, he sees every fish, never misses one,' than have him believe I'm incompetent. I have to admit, I don't always see every fish, but I reckon I see enough. Sir Laurence did once say that I was bad for his fishing because he relied on me too much. The only difference between the two of us was that I saw 75 per cent of the fish 100 per cent quicker than he did, but I'd never have admitted it.

Above us a few olives were beginning to hatch. We stopped and watched as first one bulger then another chased the emerging nymphs, catching one after another as they made for the surface. Most of these active trout were in midstream.

'They're not all killable fish,' I told Sir Laurence. 'The ones lower down are only small, no more than 1 lb or so, but the top one of the bunch looks to be the best of them. Look, see the way he pushes the water forward when he moves.'

Deciding the size of a fish by its rise or move is something that becomes easier after years of practice; it is fair to say that all three generations of Lunn have had this knack. In fact, I remember marvelling at my father's reading of a rise, and, thank goodness, it has rubbed off on me. The great thing is that it can save so much time. There's no fun in hooking an undersized fish, playing it, unhooking it and returning it to the water when all about you are other, more weighty trout ready and often willing to snatch an artificial from the surface.

Sir Laurence extended his cast and with one throw put his fly over the better of the bulging fish; it rushed upstream, like a scalded cat.

'I put him down,' he said, rather dejectedly.

It was the understatement of the year coming from Sir Laurence. Not that I mean that as a criticism: we were fishing a particularly difficult stretch of water with varying runs and currents and a pool of still water behind heaps of weed. In other words, the fish was lying in a stretch of water where it was virtually impossible to cover it well with a fly, because wherever Sir Laurence cast his fly, the line was always going to draw the fly in.

With that one failure, we walked on upstream to within sight of North Head, which was not our Beat, but as nobody was fishing it that day we were at least allowed to take a look.

It's an unwritten rule of the Houghton Club that you don't, so to speak, 'trespass' on another's water. After all, it's very annoying when you're fishing a Beat and find someone has encroached on your water. Mind you, it can happen so easily and often innocently.

In my experience after close on thirty years as Head Keeper of the Houghton Club's waters, there are two categories of fisher: the walkers and the sitters. The walker always feels that there must be a fish rising round the corner; the sitter maintains that if you sit long enough in a likely place, one fish will most surely rise. I believe the sitter wins over the walker, especially when fish are only showing occasionally. In the case of my day's play with Sir Laurence, however, the spotter always wins, just so long as he scans the water systematically and goes slowly, never moving one foot in front of the other until he has thoroughly checked the water within a few yards of him.

As we approached North Head, I suggested that Sir Laurence should rest on another of Savill's benches while I scouted the water upstream as far as Old Faithfull's hut; a now tumbled down, thatched hut erected in memory of the Head Keeper before my grandfather.

At that point the current gets under the bank as it sweeps down past Radnor's Island. It is a fairly pacy bit of water with good pots: gravel patches between the weeds where quite a few fish gather. They may not all be large fish, some may even be grayling, but there's always at least one worth a chuck.

Spotting here is also helped enormously by the shadow cast by the willows on the far bank of the island, but at that time of day the sun was progressing westward and it soon would not be any help at all.

Making sure I didn't disturb any fish ahead of me, I walked slowly, casting my eye over every inch of water from the far bank to my own. Just ahead there's a corner where I have often found a good fish, and sure enough, there was a wagging tail and a fish lying comfortably by a big water dock.

'There's a nice fish at home by the dock,' I called back to Sir Laurence.

'Do you reckon he'll take a small Red Sedge?' he asked. 'I've popped it on in readiness for the evening.'

'That'll do fine,' I called back, 'it's another of those surprise flies which can catch a lot of fish.'

'What sort of fish is he?' asked Sir Laurence as he joined me and peered into the water.

'It's no leviathan, but it's big enough. By what I saw of its tail it could be a wild fish.'

It's never easy for a right-handed caster to fish his own bank, because marginal plants have a nasty, malevolent habit of sticking out over the water. The only sure way to get the fly above the fish accurately is to cut it in under the bank, which is really only totally possible if you can cast left-handed. As a right-hander you have to make alterations to your cast to get the fly up properly to the fish.

In this instance Sir Laurence pulled line from his reel and then, with a series of false casts well outside the fish, threw a short line bang against the herbage within an inch or two of the bank. His first cast was ignored by the fish and he carefully fidgeted the fly back without getting it caught up in the vegetation.

An alternative technique is to aerialise the right length of line then cast forward, letting the rod tip drift out over the bank, which has the effect of guiding the whole line forward within inches of the bank.

'There, Sir Laurence, it rose,' I said quietly.

That move was the fish's downfall. As always, Sir Laurence's cast was superbly accurate; sheer balance and poetry in motion. And when the fish rose confidently to the fly, he timed the strike perfectly and after a short fight brought it to the net to reveal a 1 lb 11oz wild brownie: a good breakfast fish for two.

'A nice fish,' said Sir Laurence, as I released the hook, dried and treated the fly. 'It's always interested me when we've been out on these spotting days, Mick, the fish always seem to take pretty readily, even though we don't see them rise.'

'The great thing is, you can see the whole performance,' I replied, handing him his rod. 'Pop a fly over a spotted fish and if he doesn't move to it after a couple of casts, go down in size. Being able to see your fish and watch its reactions gives you a tremendous advantage. When things are quiet, the arrival of a largish fly on the surface of the water must be a tremendous temptation.'

'Rather like a fisherman on a hot day having a gin and tonic dangled in front of him,' laughed Sir Laurence.

It was getting late and the light was beginning to fade. I suggested Sir Laurence stayed where he was while I checked the last bit of water above us.

'Wasn't it somewhere along here we took a salmon a few years ago, Mick?'

'Yes, and if I remember rightly it came nicely to a shrimp pattern. This Beat was always worth a salmon or two when I was a keeper on this lower water. Mind you, in those days we used to get a fair run of salmon.'

Having checked the water above us and seen little in the way of a decent-sized fish, we headed back to Sir Laurence's car. It had been a successful day for early June, but our eyes were getting tired and it was time to head back to the Grosvenor for a drink and dinner, returning to the water in time to fish the evening rise on a new Beat. I looked for the trout I had disturbed earlier, but it wasn't at home. Maybe the brood of mallard that scurried ahead of us had scared it off again.

As we walked through the kissing gate a hundred yards upstream of the car I stopped abruptly. 'Look at that.'

There at our feet, about 3–4ft down, right on the bottom, was a good trout of at least 3 lb. I felt we were too close to do much about it and threw my cigar in the water in disgust. Blow me if the trout didn't rise and take the butt in its mouth. Sir Laurence had no need of a better invitation. He immediately crouched down and crept through the gate, got below the fish and tossed up his Red Sedge. As the fly sailed over the trout, up it came and took it.

By the way, if you are thinking of repeating the performance, you must use the correct cigar – a Castella panatella!

'How do you think we'll fare this evening?' asked Sir Laurence, as we motored through the lanes back to the Grosvenor.

'The wind seems to have backed more to the north-west, so it should die down completely,' I replied. 'It's a bit too early in the year for the blue winged olive, she won't appear before the end of June and will be the most common evening fly for the rest of the season. But with luck we should see a decent hatch of pale wateries around nine o'clock. . . .'

'And a good few rising trout if I'm not mistaken,' said Sir Laurence with obvious relish at the thought of the coming evening's sport.

Back at the Grosvenor Hotel, Sir Laurence went upstairs to the clubroom while I walked down to the rod room and weighed the catch and recorded it on the daily list. Tomorrow morning after breakfast Sir Laurence, as the senior member present, would take this list and enter the details into the book in the clubroom.

By the time I had finished entering the details of the size of fish, fly used and checked the members' rods and lines, it was time to attend to the chores across the road at the fish farm and pop home for a bite to eat so that I would be back at the Grosvenor by 7.45pm. I walked up the broad staircase to the clubroom and knocked gently on the door.

'Ah, Mick,' said Sir Laurence, nursing a glass of vintage port, 'just in time. Will you take a glass before we go back down?'

'Thank you, Sir Laurence.'

'How's the weather?'

'As I suspected, the wind has dropped and it's going to be a fine, dry evening, so it doesn't really matter where you gentlemen fish, there should be a fair chance on every Beat.'

After assigning Beats to the other members, Sir Laurence chose Coopers Meadow, a Beat in the middle water and prolific when it comes to producing fish. Coopers has a bit of everything. It's deep but not too slow at the bottom end, with a mixture of shallows and deep water above, finishing at a fine weir pool. It is sheltered to the south, east and north, but open to the west to take advantage of the fading light of the setting sun.

We parked the car at the Weed Rack Bridge, which divides Coopers from the downstream Machine Beat. The weed rack is there to catch all the floating weed which drifts down river, thus preventing it reaching the lower river and annoying members fishing that Beat. It is also a great help to keepers, because it stops the eel traps getting clogged with weed.

Fishing-wise, such a thick blanket of weed above a bridge is a great attraction, because trout love to feed on the lip where the weed forms a sort of cushion and traps floating flies.

'There ... and there ... oh that looks to be a good fish,' said Sir Laurence, as we watched trout after trout start to rise. 'But we'll have to be careful, the sun's not yet gone down and that low slanting light will mean that the fish will see us very clearly if we're not cautious and stay low.'

'We'd be better off staying here in the shade for a while, Sir Laurence,' I replied, 'it won't be long before the sun's below the horizon, then we can move upstream. There should be quite a few dead and dying spent olive and pale watery spinners after the hatch we've had this week, so a Lunn's Particular or a Yellow Boy should be a sound choice of fly.'

'That's a good fish opposite the Cable Seat,' said Sir Laurence, pointing to the spreading rings on the water.

Unlike the smart Savill benches we had passed on Upper Park Stream, the Cable Seat on Coopers was an electrical cable drum we had dragged out of the river some ten years before. It was too heavy to move further, so one of the under-keepers had turned it on its side to make a good round, comfortable seat.

The fish Sir Laurence had seen rose twice more as we moved within casting range, keeping down so that we could get as close as possible. There were quite a few natural flies coming down to the fish, so it was a little spoiled for choice. Sir Laurence covered him perfectly with a Lunn's Particular and, ignoring two naturals either side of the artificial, the trout rose so confidently it seemed as if it had been waiting for just such a fly all evening.

'Bring him downstream a bit,' I warned Sir Laurence, 'there's a nasty heap of weed upstream of me, so you need to keep the fish well away from it.'

I hate losing the first fish of the evening, but the way Sir Laurence was guiding the trout – which looked like a good one, possibly the best of the day – there was little chance it would escape.

In the net the fish weighed a touch over 3 lb. But trout were rising consistently upstream, and with the sun dipping below the horizon, flaring red and orange as it dropped behind the hill above Stockbridge, we moved on.

'There, Mick, just below the alder tree,' said Sir Laurence excitedly.

'Grayling,' I said, searching the water ahead for a likely trout. 'Let's move up towards the top of the Beat and see what's happening at the tail of the weir. There's still plenty of time before we have to move back down to the bottom of the Beat and get the best of the light for the late risers.'

Unlike the lower end of the Beat, the top of Coopers Meadow has more trees on the western bank. This puts the river into deep shadow as the light fades, so we needed to check it before it became impossible to spot catchable fish. As it was, there were occasional oncers, but no fish rising consistently to the few spent spinners drifting downstream.

Kingsmead Weir is a truly beautiful spot, perhaps one of the most picturesque stretches of water owned by the Houghton Club, and in the late evening light it has a magical quality all of its own. But if fish aren't rising, it's virtually impossible to spot them in the broken water below the weir. Later in the summer, from July onwards, it's a tremendous place for falls of sherry spinners – the spinner of the blue winged olive. These always move upstream, laying their eggs over rough water. On a good evening they gather in their thousands.

It happens all over the river, of course, at other weir pools and spots with rippling, broken water, but for me there is no sight quite like it just here, below the Kingsmead Weir. Mother Nature has probably told the flies that this is the best place for their offspring to survive, where there's plenty of life-giving oxygen.

The spinners of all our aquatic flies move upstream before egg laying, which is nature's way of making sure that all of the insects don't finish up in the sea. The sherry, though, is the most noticeable of the flies that swarm upstream to congregate over a run of broken, well-oxygenated water . . . and the fish go absolutely mad, rising continuously and all of them absolute devils to catch with an artificial. But it's good, challenging sport, nonetheless.

142

Sir Laurence Dunne brings a fish to my waiting net at Starvation Corner

'Wasn't this where Nimmo took that seven pounder, Mick?' asked Sir Laurence, recalling the June day in 1948 when Mr Nimmo, a New Zealand guest, was fishing below the weir. He took what was then the largest fish ever caught from the Houghton Club waters with a Kimbridge Sedge, one of grandfather's patterns.

Mr Nimmo, used as he was to fishing the likes of the River Tongariro and Lake Taupo, where wild brown trout run to 8 lb and more, hardly recognised the significance of such a fish. However, many past and present members of the Houghton Club would have given their casting arm for such a trout. But then, that's fishing.

'I can't believe there isn't a fish in the back eddy, Sir Laurence. I wouldn't mind £1 for every fish I've seen caught there. I'll go upstream and look down into it, the light is a touch better there.'

'Okay, Mick.'

I moved up alongside the back eddy and looked down into the water. Sure enough a few feet down a good-sized brownie was lazily picking off spinners as they tumbled round in the whirl of water. I signalled to Sir Laurence to join me. Quick off his mark and eager for another fish, Sir Laurence crept up to my side, being careful to give the back eddy a wide berth so the fish didn't catch a glimpse of him.

'Where is he?' asked Sir Laurence, peering down into the water.

'Just tight in by that willow-herb. The hatch has started, too. Pale wateries by the look of them.'

'I'll change to a Ginger Quill,' said Sir Laurence as he snapped off his Particular and nimbly tied on the new fly.

Expertly measuring his cast outside the fish, Sir Laurence let the fly fall above the fish in the choppy water inches away from where the current swirled into the back eddy, bringing the fly round quickly. It was not easy to see the fly in the fading light and broken water.

Lifting off well below the fish, Sir Laurence cast a second time. The fly swung round and the fish moved up to intercept it. 'You,' I cried, and Sir Laurence tightened into the fish as it turned down with the Ginger Quill. The fish rushed straight out across the pool, jumped and made a second headlong rush.

'What a fighter, Mick. Whoa, there it goes again. Would that every fish put up such a struggle.'

After a few hectic moments I slid the net under a 2 lb 5oz brownie.

'I think we should move downstream, Mick,' said Sir Laurence, checking his watch. 'It's getting late, and if we're going to take advantage of the light, we'd be better off fishing down near the Weed Rack Bridge.'

There were several fish showing, but it wasn't so easy to judge their size when walking downstream.

'We'll walk out round here, Sir Laurence,' I said. 'There's what looks like a decent fish by the irises, about 20 paces downstream. There, let's see him once more. There's a fly coming to him now, whoops, he missed it.'

'Just right,' said Sir Laurence as he cast the fly backhanded to the fish. It was a perfect chuck, dry fly fishing at its best, and the fish rose to it. Sir Laurence struck and, feeling the hook, the fish turned and made for the weeds upstream, taking 20 yards of line.

While Sir Laurence was playing the fish I watched the water downstream of us for other risers, but most of the fish sipping pale wateries from the surface were small wild brownies and grayling.

As Sir Laurence guided his fish to the bank, I dipped the net under the brownie and weighed it into the bag at 3 lb 2oz.

'I think we should go on downstream and see if there's a sipper at the weed rack,' I told Sir Laurence, drying his fly as we walked.

'I love the evening rise,' said Sir Laurence as we walked downstream.

'It certainly sorts the men out from the boys,' I replied.

'The damnable thing, though, is that on a good evening there can be so many fish rising you feel you could have caught any number. But with so much natural fly to choose from, they can be very pernickerty. You are also fishing against the clock.'

By now Sir Laurence's handsome Hunter showed that it was 10.30pm and the evening's fishing was virtually over.

'We'd better tie on a large Sedge for the last 15 minutes, Sir Laurence. It's such a good fly in the late evening, and, my goodness, how many times has such a fly saved a blank. As you well know, one of the best methods of fishing a Sedge is to move it across the water in much the same way the natural skitters on the surface.'

Sir Laurence held his fly to the light to fiddle his cast through the eye of the hook.

Moving a Sedge on the water is a relatively simple technique, and always a late evening fish-catcher. First, you have got to get as close to your target fish as possible, and in near darkness that is pretty close. Then, throw your Sedge outside him to the right and let the cast straighten in the stream, keeping the rod low. Then lift the rod gently so that the Sedge is against the current, which in turn induces drag.

When you see the fish rise, dip the rod tip and strike all in one movement. Dipping the rod tip, I feel, just lets the fly back into the fish's mouth. And don't be disappointed if you miss on the first strike, I've known fish come six or seven times to a Sedge fished in this 'induced drag' method.

'A lot of fishers will tell you it isn't quite cricket, you know Mick,' said Sir Laurence, a trace of humour in his voice.

'Maybe they're right, Sir Laurence, but if you are fishing to a fish you can see and such a method is the difference between catching that fish and suffering a blank, I can see no harm in it. After all, it's hellish good fun.'

As I had expected, Sir Laurence took his last fish of the evening with the induced drag. He expertly skated a large Sedge across the nose of a weed rack sipper, which popped up and took the fly as it skittered past.

'What a lovely day, Mick,' said Sir Laurence as we motored back to the Grosvenor under a full moon.

'And a perfect evening, Sir Laurence,' I agreed.

Once back at the Hotel, Sir Laurence climbed the stairs to the clubroom while I weighed and recorded the fish we had taken that evening. After a final check of the members' rods, I locked the rod room and followed Sir Laurence to the clubroom.

Inside, the members were excitedly discussing this fish or that, mixing their whiskies and gins with tales of fish caught and lost, as has been the case for more than 160 years. They settled back to an evening of discussing the fly, the fish and the flyfisher.

'Stop and have a drink, Mick,' invited Sir Laurence.

After such a splendid day in such pleasant company, and with the other members keen to talk about the day's play, I accepted. Fish, it seems, were taken on every Beat, with some fine sport enjoyed by all present. Most days on the Houghton Club waters are like that, particularly when fly are hatching and the conditions are near perfect.

But the fish and fly are not, as you can imagine, the only things members talk about after a day on the water. Like any gentlemen's club, much of the evening is taken up with stories, tall and short.

I have seldom been invited to stay on through the evening with members, who respect the fact that most mornings I'm up and out by 5am.

That evening, twenty-five years ago, was no different from countless others. As Head Keeper I was responsible for attending in the clubroom so that I could hand over the list of fish caught, where they were caught, and on what artificial, to the senior member present.

As is the tradition at the Houghton Club, I quietly handed the list to Sir Laurence. We chuckled at one entry of a brown trout weighing 1 lb 16oz taken on a Lunn's Particular.

Finishing my drink, I withdrew.

The Houghton Club is founded on tradition but that tradition does not extend to a member's academic achievement in simple mathematics.

X

LIFE IS FOR LIVING TO THE FULL

────◆◆◆────

ALTHOUGH I have lived on this river for sixty-odd years and never had any doubts that I would be anything other than a riverkeeper, I sometimes have to remind myself how lucky I am to be not just any riverkeeper, but Head Keeper of the most famous flyfishing club in the world. Not only that, I bear a name that will live on wherever the rod, line and fly are used to deceive the trout of river and lake. I just hope that if grandfather and father ever look down wistfully on the Houghton Club waters they approve of the way I have carried on the Lunn tradition of caring for the river, its wildlife, and the members of the Houghton Club.

When grandfather arrived here in 1887 he was always known as 'Lunn'; it was very much a them-and-us situation between the members and the keepers. When the anglers repaired to the Boot Inn in the village of Houghton for a midday drink, they would lunch in the saloon bar while grandfather had a glass of cider in the public bar with the chauffeurs and ghillies.

Father, too, was 'Lunn' when he started, but it soon softened to 'Alf'. In the Club's early days the clubroom was the members' 'inner sanctum', with the keeper seldom invited across the threshold. Father, however, often enjoyed an evening drink in the clubroom after a member he had been fishing with had caught a particularly large trout.

Fortunately – perhaps because I was often with my father whenever the fishing gents were around – I have always been called 'Mick'. Maybe this greater familiarity was the result of my having grown up with one generation of members – who knew me as Alf's son Mick, old Lunn's grandson – and still being here when the next generation of members came along and were introduced to me as Mick rather than Lunn. Who knows? What I do know is that this closer relationship – coupled with considerable mutual respect – has produced tremendous benefits for me and offered me a whole series of opportunities that would have been unheard of in grandfather's day and rare in father's time. How proud they would have been had they seen me some twenty years ago when I was at a shoot and drawn number eight with a peer of the realm in front of me further up the hedgerow as a stop.

In the early 1960s it was becoming increasingly evident that the Club needed to bolster its income. The most obvious way was to increase the output of the fish farm. It was the advent of commercial trout farming which changed my life completely, because my role in the Club changed from riverkeeper to trout farmer. My first job was to take on an extra keeper so that I had the time to concentrate my attention on raising and selling fish.

There were also other changes in the Test Valley and beyond, which made this move into commercial fish farming even more relevant. The river was being fished more and more; estates which had previously been fished only by the owner and his guests were being transformed into full-blown syndicate fisheries; and new lake fisheries were popping up everywhere. The demand for quality fish had never been so great.

This expansion brought me into contact with many owners of stretches of water in Hampshire and nearby counties, and lots of them needed not only fish but advice on how they could get the best out of the river they owned.

In addition to the move into commercial fish farming, I was becoming more involved in running the Club's country interests. Land and properties adjacent to the Houghton Club waters were changing hands and I was charged with keeping an eagle eye on every sale to make sure that it didn't affect the Club's rights of ownership and access.

So, in a few years, my job as Head Keeper encompassed four distinct roles: fish farmer, estate manager, overseer of all the work done by the keepers on the river, and both guide and adviser to the Club's members and guests.

This extra contact with fishermen and fishery owners has put me in touch with many, many people who have in turn offered me many kind invitations to fish and shoot with them. I have always felt that these invitations are not simply in return for services rendered but also because they thought I had a good sense of humour and was, therefore, good company.

In his days as Head Keeper my father enjoyed a few fishing and shooting trips and I remember how much I enjoyed the rare occasions when he took me with him. I loved the days when I loaded for him at local shoots, or stood by his side to pick up with the family retriever.

In the last thirty years, however, I have been given many more opportunities than ever came my father's way.

My first taste of the good life came in 1951. Years before I had dreamt of catching a salmon on a fly; I knew what it felt like to fight one of these powerful fish, having caught a kelt or two – salmon out of condition after the rigours of spawning, that were making their way back to the sea – while spinning for pike in late January and February. I had to wait until I was 25 for my boyhood dream to come true, and that through great good fortune. My father had been invited to fish for salmon at Nursling in the Test, which is a mile or so above Southampton Water. The invitation came from Mr Richard Aisher, who through father's good offices had acquired the lease on a stretch of the Test downstream of us at Mottisfont. Father suggested I went along for the ride and after I had watched them for an hour or two Mr Aisher told me to go and get a rod and fish down behind him, just for something to do.

I ran all the way to the hut and back. With trembling hands I tied on a shrimp fly and cast it out across the water. Working my way downstream I arrived at the neck of the Tree Pool and put my fly across it, watching as it swung round in the current. Then it stopped, which is more than my heart did as my whole body seemed to tingle with anticipation.

The next moment I felt the pull of a fish and we were away, with the fish first running downstream with the current, then dashing back the other way. It must have looked quite a sight with me running up and down the bank and the fish turning this way and that, trying to outwit me and get rid of the fly. But it held and about 10 minutes later the ghillie, Len Cawte, gaffed a shining, fresh-run 11 lb salmon on to the grass at my feet. Len knew it was my first fly-caught salmon, so he duly stuffed his fingers in under the gill covers and 'blooded' me. I was a 'virgin' no longer.

I have been fortunate to fish those waters on and off since I took that first salmon, thanks to the brothers Potter who have fished the water for many years, as their father did before them, but I don't think any fish since has given me quite such a thrill.

Fifteen years passed, though, before I had a chance to try for salmon in 'foreign' waters. As Head Keeper of the Houghton Club I have enjoyed the company of some fine anglers, many of whom have shown their appreciation of the job I do by offering me the chances of a lifetime, which in the ordinary course of events would never have come my way. Mr John Foster Robinson offered me one such chance of a lifetime when he invited me to fish with him on the Nith Beat just upstream of Erwood on the River Wye, about eight miles or so downstream of Builth Wells.

In the late Thirties the Wye had deteriorated so much through over-netting and other abuses that it was virtually unfishable. Through careful conservation and proper control of commercial fishing the Wye was returned to its former glory in the Fifties and today produces a larger rod catch than any other river in England or Wales.

Like any spate river the Wye is unpredictable: it runs purple-brown and is unfishable after heavy rain. Once the spate is over, though, the water can fine down within a day or two and suddenly the pools have salmon in them and the fishing is excellent. In 1989, though, the drought conditions turned what I have seen as a raging torrrent into little more than a ditch with a trickle of water in it.

Drought years have their advantages on a spate river like the Wye, particularly as it gives the keepers a chance to get out on to the river and fill the many holes and cracks in the huge, slippery rock slabs that form the river bed. Over the years, erosion has turned these rocks into what looks like huge pieces of Gruyere cheese, which makes for very tricky wading, particularly when the water is high and the current strong. In filling these holes the keepers are making it safer for the fisherman to wade.

The Nith Beat is about half a mile in length and comprises nine good salmon pools. It's an exciting place to fish, with strong running water and cauldron-like soda pools. The first year I fished it the Beat had delivered 140 fish since the start of the season five months before; I added seven to that total in only two days. I have been fortunate enough to fish with Mr John on many occasions and always looked forward to spending a few days in that wild and beautiful place.

I had my first and only visit to the Aberdeenshire Dee in 1970 as a guest of Barrie Welham, a family friend for many years. We were booked to fish Carlogie and Balogie, staying at the Portarch Hotel, but sadly the trip was cut short when I was told that my father had been taken seriously ill. I flew home immediately to discover that he had suffered a stroke. He never really recovered and died two months later: he would have been very cross at interrupting my salmon fishing, especially as it was my first visit north of the border.

The thought of having a holiday during the fishing season here never occurred to me. I know my father never did nor did any of the keepers; you were in a job which demanded that you were on parade from April until the end of September and you accepted it. Keepers in my early days took holidays beating at local shoots, although that has now changed.

Good fortune, however, came to me when I walked into the clubroom one morning in May. Commander Vivian Robinson was then the Club's honorary secretary and he casually asked me if Mr John had ever asked me to fish with him in the Outer Hebrides. He had, but I had politely turned the invitation down feeling that in July my duty was to the members of the Houghton Club and their guests. The Commander had different ideas, saying that if Mr John asked me again, I should accept, and he would answer to the other members. 'The river will be here when you come back,' he said, a twinkle in his eye.

That first trip to the Hebrides with Mr John was done in considerable style, with the party flying in a private aeroplane from Filton to Stornoway, with turkey sandwiches and gin and tonic served from take-off to landing. We were all in high spirits as we flew north and when we arrived in pouring rain a loud cheer went up; a good spate at the start of our trip was a sign that we would probably all catch fish.

We were due to stay at Morsgail Lodge overlooking Loch Morsgail, which is situated to the west of the famous Grimersta, within reach of the Morsgail River and its accompanying loch and upper river, Langavat. This is an enormous loch that the Grimersta fish run into; the Kinresort River, which runs down from Harris out of the famous Voshmidt; and the Hamnaway River with Loch Crobaig at its head. The only way to get around this wild, windswept country is by snow track, or by walking. I loved the remoteness of it, with only a golden plover for company as I walked over rock and bog, eyes turning skyward at the sight of a soaring golden eagle. Time meant nothing and after a day I couldn't have told you whether it was Monday or Friday.

I fished there with Mr John for several years until he sold. They were memorable years with marvellous fishing, but towards the end it was so heavily poached I always felt that Mr John was driven out by it.

The following year my dear friend Raymond Bushby invited Barrie Welham and me to fish with him in Iceland for a week in July. We fished the River Nordura and while the method of fishing was the same as it would be on any other salmon river, the countryside and surroundings were unforgettable. We were a pretty successful threesome: sharing two rods we caught fifty-six salmon in one week. Even more memorable were the days and nights of stories, laughter and conversation: what more could you ask for? I had only one bit of bad luck and that was on the last night in an hotel in Reykjavik prior to flying home. We tossed a coin before getting ready for dinner to determine in what order we would visit the gorgeous Icelandic blonde masseuse. I came third: she was too worn out to take me on.

After Iceland Mr John had left the Outer Hebrides, moving to the River Spey, and kindly invited me to join his party for a week's fishing. My only

151

chore, as I could see it, was driving his Bentley from Bristol to Craigellachie so that it would be available there to motor us home. I felt pretty good cruising up the M6 early one Sunday morning, until I spotted a flashing blue light in the rear-view mirror. I pulled over on to the hard shoulder and a young Brummy policeman, book in hand, asked me where I was going. I told him I was on my way to Scotland to try and catch a salmon. I asked him why he had stopped me and he explained: 'That thing under your right foot, you're pressing it too hard'. He put his book away, gave me a cheerful smile, wished me good fishing and sent me on my way.

We were fishing Delfur, which offered remarkable fishing with long, well-defined pools which from time to time held salmon in astonishing numbers. My opinion, formed after several years, is that Delfur must be the best salmon Beat anywhere in the UK. Arndilly is upstream of Delfur and up until this year was owned by another member of the Houghton Club, the Hon. A. G. Samuel. It was he, in cahoots with Mr John, who gave me a fabulous fortnight: one week as his guest at Arndilly followed by a week with Mr John at Delfur. I went to Arndilly for 10 years where I enjoyed holidays which were 'fit for a king', but sadly these are no more as the Hon. A. G. Samuel has sold up. However, I take with me memories which will keep me going forever.

Doors close but sometimes others open, and already my great friend Bill Heller has taken me to Carron and Laggan further up Speyside. Bill Heller also gave me my first and only trip to the fabulous River Gaula in Norway. We fished there during the first week of June – the President of the Houghton Club had given me full permission to be away from the Club during that time providing I caught a 40 pounder. I needed a ½ lb pebble to accomplish this because my second fish weighed precisely 39½ lb. Our party caught thirty fish with not one of them under 20 lb; it was hard, enjoyable work. There was virtually no darkness, so we fished day and night on a rota system.

Two other great friends of mine, Alan Mann and my Boston, Massachusetts buddy, Asa Allen, were responsible for yet another first: a week fishing Asa's stretch of the River Miramichi at Burnt Hill Camp in Canada. Alan and I flew to Montreal and took an internal flight to Fredericton where we met Asa. It was the end of September and the maple trees were a profusion of reds, golds and burnt orange. It was a winding and devious route, but finally we turned a sharp bend in the dirt track and there we were driving down hill, slap-bang by the river, where three guides were there to greet us. To add to my apprehension and excitement, I saw my first Atlantic salmon jump below me as I crossed the river in a canoe to the bunk house.

I can barely describe the week we spent together. It was like every 'first': a jumble of constant excitement. We caught salmon from bank and canoe using 9ft trout rods in the conventional way, casting upstream with a dry fly called a Bomber: a brown, red or green clipped deer hair concoction tied on a large size 6 or 8 hook. All you had to do was toss this beauty over a likely lie and, bingo, a rise, an instant strike and 'thar she goes'. The Miramichi in common with most Canadian salmon rivers is catch and release, with rods allowed the occasional fish for supper and the odd one for the guides' deep freeze.

My fondest memories of that trip include the day Asa organised it so that we could 'run the river', which in other parts of North America is called 'white water rafting'. We set off with three canoes and three guides loaded onto a truck and drove upstream quite a few miles. Unloading the canoes into the river where it ran near the road, we then climbed aboard and were given the most thrilling helter-skelter ride I have ever experienced; how those guides managed to steer through those high boulders and that rushing water I don't know, but it was the thrill of a lifetime.

Another memory of that trip to Burnt Hill Camp revolves around Asa's nonchalant remark that if we had any edibles we should keep them in a safe place, 'because there is a mouse or two around'. I came off the plane with just one bar of chocolate which on his advice I stored among my socks in the top drawer of my chest of drawers. In the morning half the chocolate bar was missing and there were mouse droppings all over my socks. Merlin, the head cook, guide and bottlewasher, had three old mouse traps so I set a trapline, convinced we had a plague. I baited each trap with the left-over chocolate and minutes before we left for dinner in the cookhouse there was a 'bang, bang, bang' – three mice in three traps. We reset them and after a superb meal, yes, there were three more; we killed seventeen mice in three days.

The Miramichi is God's own country: the colours of the maples improved daily and in the course of a few days I spotted a bald headed eagle, a moose, two or three deer, and a black bear, which one night broke into the foodstore. It was a memorable trip; I can still taste the pancakes and maple syrup.

Alan Mann and Asa Allen have also been generous enough to introduce me to a whole new fishing experience: angling for bonefish off the flats around the Florida Keys. It's a fascinating sport, all to do with stalking, spotting and casting accurately to a fish you can see, which is similar to a spotting day fishing Park Stream on the Houghton Club water.

Fortunately the fishing season does not conflict with the pursuit of game with the gun. Father drilled me in the rudiments and safe use of firearms, but I am largely self-taught, having progressed from shooting moorhen with a 410 to superb double-gun days at driven pheasants.

Shooting is a great social occasion, too, with news and stories being swapped between the drives and lunches that are more like banquets. Shooting, of course, is a much more organised sport than fishing. Guns foregather and are placed according to the draw. It's more like a military operation than anything else, but then so it should be; guns are dangerous things.

I have been very fortunate during the winter months to have been offered so much shooting by my fishing and fishery friends; they have all been pleasurable days, especially when I have shot well.

Like most people I have my priorities when it comes to relaxation: if there's no fishing or shooting then I go horse-racing or play golf. I have long been connected with the turf, especially on my mother's side because her cousin Bill Speck was a fine steeplechase jockey who was twice placed in the Grand National on a horse called Thomond II. For me an afternoon at the races on my rest days holds a special attraction, not least because I have sold a lot of trout to stock an owner's river, so it's pleasure mixed with a certain amount of business. I also know several jockeys who enjoy fly-fishing, though their racing tips are not always as reliable as my angling tips.

I'm not a great golfer, and at my age I'm not likely to show much improvement. Straight down the middle is my only hope, whether it be in Florida or at Sunningdale: it is a great relaxation and very rewarding.

My dear wife Joyce and my daughter Nicola (before she married) have been long-suffering, although Joyce joins in my various pursuits occasionally. Fishing is not one of her favourite pastimes: she has caught trout and salmon without really getting the bug. But she is as keen as mustard on golf. She has never understood how it is that even though fishing is my business I choose to spend most of my holidays with a fishing rod in my hand.

One of my favourite stories of the many wonderful trips I have enoyed over the years concerns Angus and the hat. On my first trip to the Hebrides a friend got himself a brand new deerstalker hat, complete with ear muffs to keep out the cold. Angus, his ghillie, never stopped admiring it: so much that my friend presented it to him at the end of our stay. The following year when my friend met Angus he noticed he wasn't wearing the deerstalker.

'Och, I haven't worn it since the accident,' he said.

'Accident?' asked my friend.

'Well,' he said, 'I was fishing on the loch on a cold morning with the ear muffs down and the Laird offered me a dram, and I never heard him.'

Weedcutting at Sheepbridge Shallows

Some accident.

Lots of water has gone under the bridge and partial, though not total, retirement looms on the horizon. I feel slightly sad that the Houghton Club has now run out of Lunns, but undoubtedly it will continue to thrive under the careful hands of those that come after me.

I am often asked if there is another Lunn who could take over from me. I explain that I have an eight-year-old grandson, Ben. But only time will tell whether Ben will be interested when he grows up. He is certainly as keen on fishing as I was at his age and he has caught his first trout and played several more.

Who knows? It has been my whole life and I have loved every single moment.

155

BIBLIOGRAPHY

An Album of the Chalk Streams
E. A. Barton
A & C Black, 1946

The Angler's Companion
Bernard Venables
George Allen & Unwin, 1958

The Birds of the British Isles
T. A. Coward
Frederick Warne, 1952

The Book of the Dry Fly
George A. B. Dewar
A & C Black, 1897

The Brook and its Banks
J. G. Wood
The Religious Tract Society, 1902

Chronicles of the Houghton Fishing Club
Edited by Sir Herbert Maxwell
The Houghton Club, 1908

Collins Field Guide to Freshwater Life
Richard Fitter and Richard Manuel
Collins, 1986

A Dictionary of Trout Flies
A. Courtney Williams
A & C Black, 1949

The Dry-Fly Man's Handbook
Frederic M. Halford
George Routledge & Sons, 1913

A Fellowship of Anglers
Horace G. Hutchinson
Longmans, Green, 1925

The Fly-Fisher's Entomology
Alfred Ronalds
Herbert Jenkins, 1836

The Freshwater Life of the British Isles
John Clegg
Frederick Warne, 1952

Over the Hills . . .
W. Keble Martin
Michael Joseph, 1968

River Keeper
John Waller Hills
Geoffrey Bles, 1934

A Summer on the Test
John Waller Hills
Hodder & Stoughton, 1924

The Way of a Trout with a Fly
George E. M. Skues
A & C Black, 1921

The Wild Flowers of Britain and Northern Europe
Richard Fitter, Alastair Fitter and Marjorie Blamey
Collins, 1974

I hope you
maintain your angle
of dangle!